Write through the Grades

Write through the Grades

Teaching Writing in Secondary Schools

Robin Bright

PORTAGE & MAIN PRESS

Portage & Main Press acknowledges the financial support of the Government of Canada through the Book Publishing Industry Development Program (BPIDP) for our publishing activities.

Printed and bound in Canada by Friesens.

LIBRARY AND ARCHIVES CANADA CATALOGUING IN PUBLICATION

Bright, Robin, 1957-
Write through the grades: teaching writing in secondary schools /
Robin Bright.

Includes bibliographical references.
ISBN 978-1-55379-122-5

1. English language—Composition and exercises—Study and teaching (Secondary)
I. Title.

LB1631.B75 2007   808'.0420712   C2007-902083-6

PORTAGE & MAIN PRESS

100 – 318 McDermot Ave.
Winnipeg, MB Canada R3A 0A2
Email: books@portageandmainpress.com
Tel: 204-987-3500
Toll-free: 1-800-667-9673
Fax-free: 1-866-734-8477

printed on 30% PCW paper

Contents

Foreword

Everyone is talented, original and has something important to say.

B renda Ueland wrote those words in a small book called *If You Want to Write,* first published in 1938. It is a book I recommend to aspiring writers; one I fondly refer to as one of my "best friends." It has served me well in my own writing and in the teaching of writing. A wise friend gave it to me as a gift.

As I read *Write through the Grades*, I realized that Robin Bright is living proof of Ueland's philosophy—as both writer and educator. So is this book. Bright's approach and understanding of the writing process with teens demonstrates that they have authentic voices and visions. Even better, this committed educator, eager to enlighten others and empower the voices of our youth, shares what she has discovered. And it is a generous sharing. We are given the benefit of her experience, research, and scholarship. We are offered her open-hearted reflections and sense a fully engaged spirit, as well as team spirit, at work. We get concrete strategies and specific exercises to encourage teen voices to find expression on the page. There are helpful suggestions on how to guide student writers through various stages and nurture excellence. Then? Bright tackles a big question: how can this creative process fit and benefit students within a system where standardized testing is "here to stay"?

Best of all, Bright lets the teens speak. Their observations of themselves as writers were, for me, often jaw-dropping. Here were insights that I am just beginning to articulate after 20 years! Their creative writing is, by turns, brilliant, funny, poignant, luminous. The "practice" is moving testimony to the theory.

I met Robin Bright on a bus trip travelling between Edmonton and Calgary one summer when we were both speakers at a literacy conference. When I heard her speak I was not just impressed, I was re-energized. Talking on the bus reassured me. I seemed on the "right" track as a teacher of writing. I bought her book *Write from the Start* and have used it in my own work ever since.

Like Ueland's, Bright's book *Write through the Grades* will become a work I call one of my "best friends." For any reader or teacher fortunate enough to discover this book, I am certain you will read it and come away feeling like I did: you have just been given a forever useful, beautiful gift by a wise friend.

Sheree Fitch, BA, MA, PhD (honours), poet, author

Acknowledgments

Writer Natalie Goldberg says that you are alone when you write a book. While this may be true, I did not write this book without the support and assistance of others. I am indebted to the many fine teachers who have invited me into their classrooms to observe, teach, and talk about writing instruction. In particular, I thank Carrie Netzel and Lola Major, two teachers I have long admired and respected, for sharing their time, their insights, and knowledge with me throughout the writing of this book. Also, thanks go to teachers Maureen Swanson-Warren and Mary-Ann Gajdostik for their support with my research.

I would like to thank my friends and colleagues in the Literacy Research Centre at the University of Lethbridge, Michael Pollard, Pamela Winsor, Cynthia Chambers, Erika Hasebe-Ludt, and Leah Fowler for their continued collegiality, wisdom, and shared passion for language and literacy.

Thanks also to the eight talented and intelligent students with whom I worked over four years while studying their habits and perceptions about writing and its instruction. Their words grace the pages of this book, and I wish them much success and a lifelong love of writing.

I am fortunate to have had the benefit of working with careful readers of my work—Marg Joblonkay, Barb Krushel, Carol Dahlstrom, and the staff at Portage & Main Press, because almost all good writing begins with terrible first efforts.

I am grateful to my parents, Sheila and Ed Ryan, both avid readers and writers, for their love and support.

Finally, I would like to thank Glenn, Amy, and Erin, who have never wavered in their support for the work I love to do, and who have taught me about love, patience, and, above all, good humour.

Introduction

One of my most vivid memories of writing in school occurred in Mr. Hunter's grade-8 classroom. A tall, thin man with a short, straight-standing brush cut, Mr. Hunter came to teaching as a second career. We suspected that his first had been in the military because of the haircut, but, in those days, you did not ask. Mr. Hunter was a little older than my other teachers; however, his age did not interfere with his enthusiasm for language. He loved teaching English! He always carried a book and read to us on a regular basis. He was genuinely excited when he introduced writing assignments, and his enthusiasm rubbed off on us, his students.

In the 1970s, writing instruction was predominantly a product-oriented endeavour. Mr. Hunter would come to class with several ideas for us to consider. Then, when he assigned the writing task, he would provide some class time for us to work on it, but it was understood that most of our writing would be done as homework.

Mr. Hunter arrived one day with a stack of our writing assignments in his hand. These he had marked the previous evening. He was his usual enthusiastic self, smiling and complimenting our efforts. Then, he read aloud Veronica's piece. Stuck in my memory ever since is the following sentence: "The sickeningly sweet smell of juicy fruit gum wafted throughout the classroom." Wow! I remember thinking. What a brilliant line. I did not think I could ever write something as good as that, and that day I gave up all thoughts of ever being a writer.

My interest in writing, however, was re-ignited later on, during my 10 years of classroom teaching. Observing and working with 6- and 7-year-olds, I was fascinated by their attempts to use all kinds of writing—drawings, scribbles, lines, zigzags, letter-like formations, and even words, spelled phonetically or by sight—to record their ideas, thoughts, and seemingly never-ending stories. Without much instruction, but with lots of encouragement, my students seemed to love opportunities to write and draw. When I asked them to tell me what they had been writing, they did so eagerly, articulately, and confidently. I often focused on writing instruction with these young students. I read the work of Donald Graves, Lucy Calkins, Nancie Atwell, Glenda Bissex, among others, and tried many new teaching strategies. During my graduate work, I researched the topic of teaching writing and read widely about authors who spoke about how and why they write. (Looking back, I think this focus on writing may have been an unconscious attempt to understand why I did not think of myself as a writer in school.)

Years later, when I was completing my doctoral studies at the University of Victoria in British Columbia, I had the good fortune to work with a group of middle-school students and ask them about their views about the value of the writing they were doing (see Bright, *Writing*). To find out how a student viewed the value of writing in his or her life, I would always ask the following question, which quickly got to the heart of the matter: "Let's say that tomorrow morning, when you wake up, just about everything in your life is the same as it is right now. You wake up in the same house, dress in your own clothes, and go to your regular school. But there is one thing that is different about you. Tomorrow, when you wake up, you can no longer write. Would it matter to you?"

As might be expected, several of these middle-school students talked about writing as a way to deal with problems and issues in their lives. Others talked about writing as an ability they had acquired that helped them to learn. Still others said that they would miss being able to communicate with friends and family. Several had a hard time articulating what they would miss were they unable to write. Donald, a straight-shooting boy of 11, considered my question for a moment or two. He then looked me in the eye and asked, "Could I still write cheques?" When I said that he could, he told me that not being able to write, then, would not matter to him. Donald's response started me thinking about what we as educators were teaching about writing in our schools. My recollections of what Mr. Hunter hoped we would learn in grade 8 reinforced Robert Gundlach's idea that "there is at best an indirect relationship between what children are taught about writing and what they learn" (134).

Effective writing instruction began to flourish in elementary schools in the 1980s, when we started using such strategies as brainstorming, webbing, writers workshops, editors tables, self-editing checklists, writing to real audiences, and self-selected topics for writing. I was fortunate to be teaching school during those years, first as a grade-1 teacher and then as a grade-4 teacher. I continued reading books and journals on writing, attended professional conferences, and documented the results of my own teaching practices through ongoing professional development and research. Through it all, I was amazed and fascinated by young children's writing. They appeared fearless in their attempts to make their thoughts known—through quick rewrites, stories, reports, and in journals, letters, and portfolios. Even struggling writers showed enthusiasm when given a writing assignment that caught their interest; they often wrote passionately, if only briefly, on that topic. When I decided to pursue a doctorate in education, I knew that my research would involve the teaching of writing in schools. I enjoyed learning from students.

During the past decade, I have done research, published, and spoken publicly about writing instruction in the primary and elementary grades, focusing on children's earliest literacy experiences with writing and any printed material that they come into contact with, in storybooks, on signs, or even their own names (see: Bright, *Writing*; Bright, McMullin and Platt; Bright, *Write*). My colleagues and I at the university and in schools observe and work with students on a regular basis through research, guest teaching, presentations, workshops, and conferences to help improve literacy instruction for children and youth. We try to discover and then put into practice the most effective ways of teaching children to write (Tompkins, Bright, Pollard, and Winsor).

It was not until the last few years, however, when my eldest daughter was in middle school and then high school, that I began to understand that researching student writing was important not only in the elementary grades. I came to realize, as Michael Pressley points out, that the writing development of a 12-year-old in middle school or a 17-year-old in high school should be as critical a concern to our society as the writing development of a preschool or an elementary-school child. However, as Donna Alvermann indicates, literacy research in the upper grades often goes unnoticed by policy-makers and the general public. This is occurring at a time when fewer students than ever are reaching basic levels of achievement in reading and writing.

Many middle- and high-school students have decided, just as I had in Mr. Hunter's classroom, that they are not writers. My own conversations with middle- and high-school teachers indicate that they, too, struggle with trying to encourage and inspire older students to want to write. As well, these teachers feel pressure to ensure that their students have met specific government-mandated curriculum and achievement-test standards in writing. These standards involve achievement in writing content, organization, sentence structure, vocabulary, and mechanics. Future writing instruction must take into consideration teens' views of themselves as writers, their motivations, and their backgrounds and interests, as well as the experiences and backgrounds of their teachers, not to mention the pressures under which they work.

With these goals in mind, more recently I have begun studying writing instruction in middle schools and high schools. In 2001, I began a research project, funded in part by the University of Lethbridge Teaching Development Department, with eight 14-year-old students and four teachers, to examine their views about writing and its instruction in school. These students were identified as "exemplary writers," meaning that they chose to write on their own, they enjoyed writing, they were good at it, and they valued writing in their lives. I hoped that, by working with a group of writers like this, and their teachers, I could devlop ideas to improve writing instruction for all adolescents, most of whom report that they write less, and enjoy doing it less, as they get older.

This book documents my research into writing instruction and my work with these students and their teachers over a four-year period: from their grade-9 year to their final year in high school. By both looking at the scholarly literature on writing instruction and listening to what the teens themselves said, I found a strong connection between the theory and practice of teaching writing. The teens' comments about their writing habits and preferences provided us with some solid and thought-provoking suggestions for how and why to teach writing. It is my belief that teaching writing can be far richer and more extensive when we listen to teens talk about learning to write than if we relied on research alone.

The purpose of this book is to ensure that researchers and teachers do not abandon the efforts of those before them who helped document and improve writing instruction from its early product-oriented days to its present-day context, which focuses on process, fluency, and choice.

I was fortunate that two very experienced teachers, Carrie Netzel and Lola Major, agreed to continue our work and discussions about writing even after the study came to a close. Carrie participated in the study as a colleague who identified one of the student writers and then participated with me in discussions about teaching writing during the four years of the study. Lola, a recently retired teacher, joined our professional discussions during the last two years of the study. Lola and Carrie, too, have a deep and abiding interest in adolescent literacy generally and writing specifically, and they were willing to share their experiences as educators to contribute to this book. Lola and Carrie provided the writing assignments and the student writing samples found in chapter 6. Through the writing of this book, I am committed to helping teen writers find their voices and use writing in meaningful and thoughtful ways both in school and throughout their lives.

Looking Back,
Looking Ahead

Sad to say, the research community is paying less attention to writing these days than was true a decade ago.... It is evident that we can teach students to write better, and that writing can benefit content learning, but we would benefit from much more detailed analyses of how to do these things more effectively. (Shanahan 73)

Goal of this Chapter

My goal in this chapter it to present: (1) an overview of the history of writing instruction research; (2) a summary of reasons to focus on writing in school and in the larger society; (3) an introduction to The Writing Process and its stages; and (4) a discussion of the challenges of teaching writing to teens and suggestions for future directions in teaching the discipline of writing in middle and high schools.

In today's world, being able to write effectively contributes enormously to a person's ability to successfully navigate life's demands and expectations. For example, it allows us to compose newsletters, memos, and emails at work or write cards and thank-you notes in our personal lives. Writing lists helps us organize our thoughts and our daily routines. Writing journals and diaries helps us clarify our thoughts and emotions. Writing notes and recording facts and figures helps us make sense of a lecture or a book. Writing provides some of us with opportunities to express ourselves creatively—in poetry or prose, for example. Unfortunately, however, few people graduating from high school can confidently say that they view themselves as competent writers, and few teachers would admit to writing on a regular basis.

HISTORY OF THE RESEARCH

Many students in the 1960s and 1970s experienced writing in school as a subject that was assigned rather than taught. Teachers were primarily concerned with what the students produced in response to an assignment.

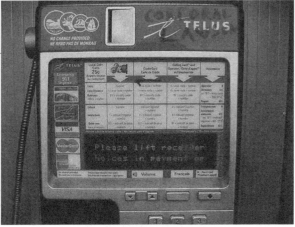

—In today's world, being able to write effectively contributes enormously to a person's ability to navigate life's demands and expectations.

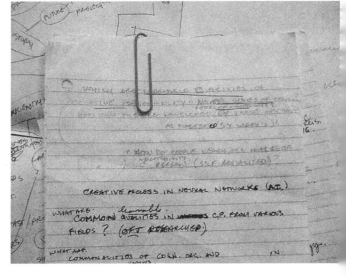

Writing assignments were usually restricted to English and social studies courses, and only sometimes given in science and psychology. It was not considered important how the students arrived at a final product but simply that they handed in some writing when it was due. Donald Murray, an English professor at the University of New Hampshire, himself a writer, is one scholar who refers to this kind of writing instruction as "product-oriented." Often the result of product-oriented instruction was that teachers viewed students as coming into their classrooms already designated as either superior writers or as inferior writers—you either had it or you did not. Because whole-group instruction was the norm in the 1960s and 1970s, little or no time was devoted to instructing the individual student on his or her writing. Product was more important than process. It is not surprising, then, that writing was viewed as a somewhat mysterious process that people were either naturally suited to or not. This view is in stark contrast to Elaine Farris Hughes's recent observation: "I'm convinced that most people are born story tellers and that the act of writing can be a pleasure" (3).

Over the past 25 years, teachers and researchers have made great strides in helping us understand what writers are doing when they write. This information has led to changed and improved writing instruction that better meets the learning needs and interests of students. In particular, it is now recognized that writers use a specific process when they write, consisting of a series of stages that includes prewriting, drafting, revising, editing, and publishing. Knowing these stages and the strategies that are used at each stage assists teachers and students to better understand how to go about writing. Knowing about the process of writing serves as well to demystify for the student writer what needs to occur between the time when a writing task is assigned and when it is handed in.

It cannot be said that all, or even a majority, of teens (and even adults) like to write. It seems incongruous that, despite the vast amount of research about the process of writing throughout the 1980s and 1990s, by researchers and teachers alike (including Nancie Atwell, Donald Graves, Lucy Calkin, Michael Pressley, Robert Tierney, and Linda Rief), "there is still very little teaching of high school students about how to compose" (Pressley 428). Pressley's research points to the shortcomings of writing instruction in middle and high school:

> Many middle and high school students do not know how to compose well. For some, it is a lack of higher order skills—not knowing how to plan, draft, and revise a paper. For others, however, it is a lack of lower order skills—not knowing grammar or mechanics well, so that most sentences written by such students have problems with them. In addition, many middle and high school students cannot spell. (422)

One reason that writing is not improving among secondary students is that teaching writing is often relegated to the English teacher alone. Educators and their students are beginning to understand that writing instruction should not be confined to the English classroom. The benefits to teachers, when they incorporate writing assignments into such other disciplines as social studies, science, mathematics, computer technology, and drama, for instance, are far-reaching. In their students, according to Robert Tierney, there is:

- an improvement of their general writing ability
- an increase in their understanding of new content
- acquisition of specific vocabulary
- stimulation of critical thinking and creativity

There is, then, a clear need for teachers in all disciplines to teach writing in their classrooms. Teachers need to help their students increase their writing fluency and learn the skills necessary for producing effective writing, including content, vocabulary, sentence structure, organization, and mechanics.

THE WRITING PROCESS

Due to a surge of research conducted over the past 30 years, a great deal is now understood about writing and about teaching writing. Beginning in 1971 with Janet Emig's seminal study of grade-12 students, teachers and researchers have looked at the processes involved in writing. Emig observed several good high-school writers while they engaged in producing a piece of writing, which was a departure from the product-oriented approach to writing instruction that had previously dominated. Not only did Emig observe these grade-12 students, but she also asked them questions about their thinking and the steps they followed. What resulted was the beginning of what we have come to know as The Writing Process. Emig concluded that good writers go through the following stages:

- prewriting (planning)
- drafting (quickly getting ideas written without regard for correctness)
- revising (rereading, reorganizing, finding the best leads)
- editing (focusing on language mechanics)
- publishing (sharing with others)

Researchers and teachers at all levels began to use the stages identified by Emig. Many began contributing to knowledge about The Writing Process by documenting students' behaviours and their writing as they worked. Shelley Peterson's circular depiction of The Writing Process shows its flexibility to meet a writer's individual approach (see figure 1.1). Donald Murray, in his article entitled "Writing as Process" puts it this way:

> This new interest in the process of writing, rather than the product of writing, opens the doors for important and interesting research which can employ all of the tools of intelligent research. It is a job which needs to be done.... The better we understand how people write—how people think—the better we may be able to write and to teach writing. (101)

Once it became known and accepted that writers engage in a series of steps as they write, it seemed logical that teachers could use that information to guide their instruction. Many teachers began teaching their

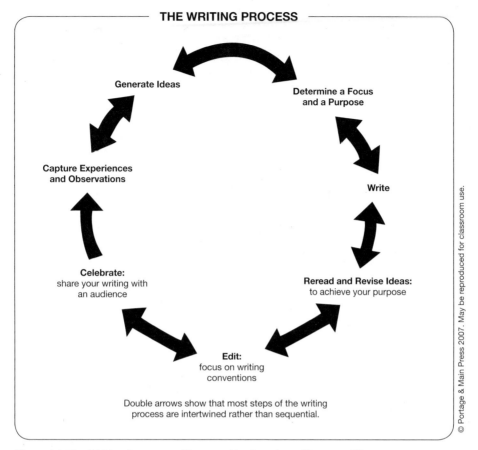

THE WRITING PROCESS

Generate Ideas

Determine a Focus
and a Purpose

Capture Experiences
and Observations

Write

Celebrate:
share your writing with
an audience

Reread and Revise Ideas:
to achieve your purpose

Edit:
focus on writing
conventions

Double arrows show that most steps of the writing
process are intertwined rather than sequential.

Figure 1.1. The Writing Process as illustrated in chart form (Peterson 12)

students the names of the stages and strategies to be used within each. Teacher-made and commercially produced posters identifying The Writing Process sprang up in classrooms, and students learned to associate certain strategies and behaviours with each stage.

DRAWBACKS TO USING THE WRITING PROCESS

The Writing Process is a tremendous help to those of us interested in learning about and teaching writing. However, there are some difficulties associated with it, and these must be taken into account when we talk about teaching writing to adolescents. One difficulty is the interpretation of The Writing Process as a formula for producing good writing. Another lies in the simplistic nature of a defined process; it does not address all the complexities of learning to write.

The Writing Process as Formulaic

The introduction of The Writing Process in schools was a breakthrough. It provided a much-needed structure that teachers could use to organize their programs. It helped students who struggled with getting started and students who felt stuck. However, it was often seen as too formulaic. It asked students to follow a predetermined pattern. For instance, teachers would reserve Mondays for prewriting, Tuesdays and Wednesdays for drafting, Thursdays for revising and editing, and Fridays for recopying into a published piece. The formulaic approach, however, often inhibited students' writing development. Learning to write is often a messy process of discovery; a formulaic approach can impede this process.

Many writers have talked about how they follow the stages of The Writing Process, and they use the process in very diverse ways. For instance, Sarah Ellis, an author of books for young adults, says that she spends a great deal of time prewriting (researching and reading) but does not differentiate the later stages from one another. For her, it is counter-productive to separate them. Another well-known author of books for young adults, Kit Pearson, indicates that she does a lot of research in the prewriting stage but, once she begins drafting, does not go back and examine those prewriting notes. These two published writers said that the revision stage is paramount, and others supported this approach—they said that there is no writing without revision, some going as far as to say that writing is 90 percent revising. These examples indicate that there is a need for flexibility in any writing process and that we need to modify Emig's process in our current teaching methods.

The Writing Process as Simplistic

Emig's work occurred at the same time as that of other researchers, including Linda Flower and John Hayes's "Plans that Guide the Composing Process," Donald Murray's "Writing as Process" and George Hillocks's *Research on Written Composition,* who were demonstrating the complexity of the writing process. Together, their work helped teachers and writers understand that writing is far from a straightforward act. A writer does not simply sit down and effortlessly write what he or she intends. Rather, producing the desired outcome requires in-depth analysis, complex synthesis, and multiple attempts. For example, analyzing a piece of writing involves reading and rereading material that may be related to the writing (or the piece itself). Synthesis is the constant putting together of ideas, information, and words that reveal the writer's thoughts. Teaching students to engage in this kind of complex activity is not a simple task. There is evidence to suggest that, in order to participate in writing at this higher level, students need to follow some guidelines. Timothy Shanahan found that students need to:

- be involved in frequent opportunities to write
- take a perspective when they write
- use revision throughout the writing activity
- personalize the writing in some way
- have their writing needs evaluated

Shanahan's findings stand in opposition to findings by other researchers. Arthur Applebee discovered, in his work in high-school settings, for example, that most writing by students on a day-to-day basis is of short answers to test questions or questions following a reading. He found that students were not using writing to tackle the difficult questions in their learning. Instead, they were using it in its simplest form—rote learning. Yet, his work with Judith Langer demonstrates that, when students engage in the complex activity of writing, they are involving very specific thinking skills and abilities that are unique to writing itself.

We have learned from early research that the longer the form is (e.g., a novel), the longer will be the recall of complex information. Furthermore, we know that the introduction of longer forms of writing must be accompanied by a teacher-student discussion about the purpose of the writing and how students should engage in the writing in order for it to be effective. It is not enough for a teacher to assign writing tasks to adolescents; there must also be time set aside for discussion about what the students will be doing. Unfortunately, some early interpretations of The Writing Process do not take into account the important role of discussion in developing students' writing abilities.

LOOKING AHEAD

No one would deny the importance of the research done over the past 30 years about the process of writing. However, if we are to continue to move forward in our understanding of how writers develop, the focus now needs to be on the perceptions of individual students and on the education of teachers about how to teach writing.

The writing that teens do is embedded in a variety of complex tasks called "the new literacies." According to researcher Bertram Bruce, the new literacies refer to a person's use of language while surrounded by vast resources of information—the Internet, media, and ever-changing technologies, for example. I view learning to write not as a solitary act but one that is affected by these new literacies. The teachers and the teens I worked with and write about in this book live in a world of rapidly changing literacies, and they must be viewed as constantly adapting to these literacies in their daily lives, both in and out of school.

Past research clearly shows that knowledge of The Writing Process can help a struggling student get started on a piece, for example. And an understanding of the process can help teachers who are uncertain about how their students move from receiving an assignment to completing it. However, it is important to ensure that the process not be used in a formulaic or a simplistic manner. My experience and research clearly point to three specific ways that middle- and high-school teachers can do this: (1) use writers workshops (2) listen to what writers (students and experienced writers alike) say about their writing, and (3) understand the role of compliance and resistance in writing.

Writers Workshops

One excellent way in which teachers can put theory about writing into practice is by offering writers workshops. Nancie Atwell is considered one of the gurus of using writers workshops for adolescents. In her book *In the Middle,* she describes how she presents writers workshops in her classrooms and suggests how other teachers can do the same. She describes how to help students find their own topics for writing, set up routines necessary to maintain the workshop momentum, and use conferences; she provides mini-lessons for teaching a variety of topics related to writing.

One of the most important aspects of a writers workshop is that of helping students find their own topics for writing, which in turn helps them develop ownership of their work and value writing as an important part of their lives. This aspect appeals to adolescent students; it is an opportunity for them to spend time on subjects that really matter to them.

Students in the workshop setting need to be provided with uninterrupted time for writing. This enables them to work at their own individual paces (whether they are prewriting, drafting, revising, editing, or publishing) and receive assistance from the teacher when they need it. The teacher acts more as a facilitator than as a lecturer. Older students, especially, thrive in this atmopshere, as they will have had more experience working independently. As part of their instruction in writers workshops, teachers should use conferences extensively. These can occur between teacher and student(s) or among two or more students.

Research shows that, while they are time-consuming, writers workshops are more beneficial than any other teaching method for improving student writing and helping students develop an interest in writing. (See chapter 3 for a sample writers workshop.)

What Writers Say about Writing

A great deal has been written about the processes that published writers follow and how their experiences can be used to teach students. Some accounts have been provided by the writers themselves, and others have been guided by researchers. One of the most important conclusions in this research is that writing is a highly idiosyncratic process. No two writers approach their work in exactly the same way. Nonetheless, there are some similarities that are worth mentioning. For example, many writers talk about the importance of their physical settings to writing, and, while they may not agree on aspects of the environment that are conducive to writing, they all say that they have certain patterns of behaviour, protocols, and routines that they require in order to write.

Donald Murray, in his book entitled *A Writer Teaches Writing*, was one of the first writers to fully examine and explicate his own writing processes for an audience of researchers, teachers, and writers. He believes that there is no one way to write and that each writer approaches the endeavour in a way that makes sense to him or her. Murray describes the process of writing this way:

> Writing starts in the middle or the end or the beginning of the process. It starts where it starts. And you use the process in whatever way it can help you make an effective piece of writing. (101)

Writers use the stages of The Writing Process in highly individual ways, and, likewise, teachers of writing need to provide a variety of strategies. For example, after teachers have talked to students about the prewriting stage generally, they need to ask students to reflect on their own prewriting strategies. The teacher might also share his or her own prewriting strategies. This lets students know that prewriting can be approached in different ways, depending on the writer, the purpose of the writing, and the audience.

The opinions of writers about their writing may differ from those of teachers of writing. Chris Crowe examined several writing textbooks used in schools and noted what was emphasized in them, then identified a number of elements that published writers say are often overlooked in the teaching of writing in schools. Eleven of these are:

1. reading widely
2. writing daily
3. attending to deadlines
4. writing subconsciously
5. using the computer
6. writing the lead first
7. writing anywhere
8. writing in a quiet atmosphere
9. knowing the purpose
10. being flexible with rules
11. asking peers to edit

Research such as Crowe's shows that there are aspects of writing instruction that are not congruent with the practices of published writers. Given these findings, we need to encourage teachers to have their students talk or write about the process of writing. Teachers also should share their own experiences as writers with their students, even admitting to their own feelings of reluctance and ambivalence. Teachers will find that they learn about writing alongside their students.

Compliance and Resistance in Writing

The work of Peter Elbow is helpful in any discussion of the challenges and successes of writers. He says, "What got me interested in writing was being unable to write" (5). In order to address his own writing difficulties in university, Elbow was able to identify two important forces at work when one writes. He says that there exists an inherent (and necessary) conflict between the desire to comply and the desire to resist. According to Elbow, one problem with students' writing is that someone (or something) other than the writer is always in charge—the teacher, the assignment, or the criteria. Therefore, there is a great deal of pressure to comply.

This was certainly the experience of a grade-2 student being observed by researcher Anne Haas Dyson in her classroom. The student was being observed because of her keen interest in writing. She wrote pages and pages in response to any topic suggested by her teacher. One day, Dyson observed the student erasing and changing some of her writing. Unsure about the nature of the changes she was making, Dyson asked her what she was doing. She confided quietly that she knew that the next day was the day for editing their writing and correcting their mistakes, but, because she did not make any mistakes, she was putting some errors into her writing so that she would have something to correct. This young girl complied so well to her teacher's expectations that she did not develop a true understanding of why one engages in the revision process.

The opposite of compliance, according to Elbow, is resistance. As teachers of writing, we all know students who resist our attempts to get them to write. This is a very powerful stance for a student to take. Have you ever tried to make someone write? The strongest form of resistance is to not write at all; another is to write badly or to not care about the writing. However, in a more positive vein, resistance can mean coming up with one's own purpose, one's own reasons, for writing. The trick is for teachers to find ways to get students to do their writing assignments diligently and willingly, yet maintain their independence and autonomy as writers. We must find ways to get students to both comply and resist.

The Study:
What Teens Tell Us

As teachers, most of us say we want our students to develop some authority of voice, yet many of our practices have the effect of making students more timid and hesitant in their writing. (Elbow 205)

Goal of this Chapter

My goal in this chapter is to share the results of a four-year study that followed eight teens who were identified by their teachers as exemplary writers. The students were 14 years old at the beginning of the study and 17 at the end. I present the participants' profiles, interview data, and the research questions that brought out the participants' views, habits, and perceptions about effective writing instruction.

As my own interest moved from teaching young children to write toward teaching teens to write, I was encouraged by Michael Pressley's work on secondary-school literacy education. Pressley tracked the time that middle- and high-school students spent writing in school and observed the kinds of writing they were asked to do. His findings indicated that there is very little time spent in school teaching teens *how* to write and suggests that greater attention be paid to helping teachers find out what teens can do as writers so that worthwhile instruction strategies can be developed. My own interest matched Pressley's, and I started talking with two middle-school teachers and two high-school teachers with whom I had worked in the past and who had expressed an interest in doing research in this area. We soon embarked on a collaboration that turned into a formal study entitled "Learning about Writing Instruction: What Teens Tell Us." Each of my four colleagues identified one or two students who demonstrated strong writing competence. We hoped that talking with and observing exemplary student writers in middle school and high school would provide us with important insights into effective writing strategies. We talked about a number of studies whose authors had examined the composing processes of good writers, including Janet Emig's earlier study of eight grade-12 students. These four teachers and I worked together, alongside the eight teen writers identified as exemplary, for one year. After that, only two of the teachers remained in the study.

Author and University of British Columbia creative writing teacher Steven Galloway says that writers often learn things about themselves and about writing simply by having the chance to talk about the subject. In an interview conducted by Kathy English in the *Globe and Mail* in May 2003, he says, "The things you find you know by virtue of being forced to articulate them constantly amaze me." Working with this group of students over four years had the same effect on me, and we are satisfied that we have significantly added to the body of knowledge about teaching writing by clearly identifying the type of instruction that works for students and teachers alike.

During our initial discussions, my colleagues and I decided that we wanted to find out how exemplary teen writers think about writing, how they view themselves as writers, and how they perceive the writing instruction they receive in school. When we began the study, the students were in grade 9 and were 14 years old. I remained in touch with them from middle school and throughout high school, corresponding with each of them one final time when they entered grade 12. I felt that their comments, over the four-year period, would give us useful information about effective writing practices for middle- and high-school student writers.

Based on these goals, we designed a set of four questions, which I asked during the course of three interviews with them. One interview was held at the beginning of their grade-9 year, a second was held at the beginning of their grade-10 year, and a third (conducted as a questionnaire by email) was held at the end of their grade-12 year. The same four questions were asked each time, and the responses were examined in terms of how they compared over time. The questions were:

1. What influences led to your interest in and aptitude for writing?
2. Which instructional practices, in and out of school, have been helpful to you? Which practices have been unhelpful?
3. What are your writing habits in and out of school?
4. What do you think is the value of writing?

These questions also served as an organizing structure for discussion of the findings.

At the end of the four years, I mailed a final ("exit") questionnaire to each of the students so that I could obtain current information about their perceptions. I also asked them to submit a piece of writing that they had produced within the previous six months, which represented their current writing abilities.

The two teachers and I discussed and shared many of the teachers' writing assignments, students' writing samples, marking rubrics, literature used to encourage writing, and instructional strategies. We also talked about the students in the study, observed their writing, and offered insights into what contributed to their interest in and aptitude for writing. These conversations were an important source of information for me, as we discussed many aspects of how they taught writing—both the joys and the challenges.

THE PARTICIPANTS

Eight 14-year-olds (six girls and two boys), together with four teachers —two at the middle-school and two at the senior-high-school level— participated throughout the study. (Throughout the four-year study, I remained in contact with only one of the four original teacher-participants—one teacher became ill, and another found it difficult to get to the campus because she lived some distance away. The teacher who remained was Carrie Netzel, and we were later joined by Lola Major, a newly retired teacher, and the three of us carried on informal face-to-face and electronic conversations.) The original teachers and students were from four different school districts, including both rural and urban districts, in the province of Alberta. The participants were chosen because they were considered by their teachers to be very good writers. The teachers based their decisions on the marks in writing from the provincial achievement tests and on daily observations of the students. In order to look at the students' writing development over time, we remained in contact over four years, until the eight students were in grade 12 and were 17 years old. I obtained the students' and their parents' permission to participate in the study. I interviewed each of the students twice within the four-year period, first when they were 14 and then when they were 16. A graduate student assisted in transcribing and analyzing the interviews. I asked the participants to save copies of the writing they did over the course of the study, and I used samples of their writing as a focal point during the interviews.

Jamie

Jamie was a tall, slim, and slightly reserved student of 14 when the study began. She became animated when speaking about her interest in writing. At the beginning of the study, she attended a medium-sized Catholic junior high school and, later, a large public high school. Jamie talked about her habit of writing outside of school on a regular basis and told me she was working on a novel—one she hoped would reach between 200 to 300 pages. Jamie said that her interest in writing had developed over the previous two years, beginning in grade 7. At that time, she was particularly interested in writing stories and poetry. When asked why, Jamie said, "I think it was along the lines of junior high, coming here is sort of stressful, makes you want to do something different. Get your mind off those things at school." Jamie wrote at home for personal reasons, but she also wrote effectively at school. Clearly, her personal writing enhanced her development as a successful writer in school.

Jamie was aware of her own writing processes. She talked knowledgeably about the planning stage and about brainstorming and thought-webs. She also said that she did not spend much time prewriting but preferred to begin drafting right away. It was evident from my interviews with her that Jamie was thinking about topics, plots, and even vocabulary on an ongoing basis. For her, a more difficult part of writing was "trying to find really interesting words to use, different ones." Jamie talked about planning, drafting, revising, and publishing, but, in the end,

Amongst the Soldiers

His hands trembled as he pulled the letter out of the mail compartment.

Jonathan Kent stood with his wife in the small post office. They were newlyweds as of only two weeks ago, and never regretted their commitment. They loved each other dearly; as the vows go, "Till death do us part."

It had been one week since they had checked their new mail compartment, and already they had a letter. Yet Jonathan felt there was something wrong with this one, something was going to happen.

The letter was addressed to him.

"What does it say?" his wife, Maria, asked.

Jonathan shook his head silently as he tore open the envelope. He unfolded the letter and read it aloud.

Dec 10, 1941

Dear Jonathan Mitchell Kent,

The Canadian militia requires your attendance in our recent war, in which many countries are involved, in the fight against Germany. We've many recruits from a number of allied countries, yet we need more intelligent highly trained recruits. Our government would highly approve of your assistance, for you will be a great asset to our fight, for not only ours but many countries. This is a very important matter and we greatly need your patriotism.

Please report to your nearest headquarters by December 15, 1941.

Sincerely,

General Carlson Weiter

—A sample of Jamie's writing in response to a Remembrance Day assignment in her English language-arts class

she credited being able to write as an ineffable quality: "You have to have the heart to do it." She was familiar with a variety of genres (science fiction, fantasy, and realistic fiction were her favourites), and she felt she was best suited to writing fiction.

Jamie credited her teacher with helping her with the mechanics of writing, such as punctuation. She suggested that her own interest in reading was helpful for developing ideas for writing. Jamie reads three or four books a month. She identified several favourite authors and book titles when asked what she liked to read. She said she liked Terry Brooks's novels, especially *The Sword of Shannara Trilogy*, for the effective descriptions of setting and character. Jamie spoke about the importance of her mom as a reader of her writing: "She is very happy that I love to write. She's proud of me." Jamie also said she had a close friend who supported and encouraged her.

Holly

Holly, a tall, confident, and reflective 14-year-old, spoke about writing in a straightforward and thoughtful manner. She attended a public junior high school and then a large public high school with 1000 students. Her family relocated temporarily, and she spent her grade-12 year at a high school in Florida. From the outset of the interviews, Holly had identified herself as a writer and spoke about her strengths and weaknesses with knowledge

From the Diary of Eliza Moon

Friday, May 31st, 1996

Locker doors slammed shut. The halls of Lakeview High School were busy and bustling. Students were running to get to their first class. I grabbed my books and rushed to my first class, science, the furthest classroom away from my locker. I sighed and started walking. There was a tap on my shoulder. I turned to see Lana, my best friend, jog up beside me.

Lana, with her beautiful blonde hair bouncing and her amber eyes dancing, turned not just a few heads when she walked down the hall. For all her good looks, you would think she'd be the most popular girl in the school. But I was her only friend. It seemed that her good looks actually turned the other girls against her. So when the girls turned against her, the boys befriended her (I have also been Lana's friend since elementary school and that wasn't about to change). Having the attention of the boys made the other girls even angrier, so Lana (and I) were alienated and a small school war was brewing.

On our way up the stairs, we walked past Janice (the leader of the "Lana-hater's gang") and Lana smiled her biggest smile.

"Good morning, Janice." Janice glared at us and double-timed it up the stairs ahead of us to fire up the rest of the gang. It was a wonder that Janice had so much power over so many girls, with her bad attitude, but that's the way it is sometimes.

"Lana, don't do that, it's only making them angrier," I whispered. One day Lana was going to get way more than a nasty note from the gang if she kept being that nice to them. Okay, I know that sounds pretty funny, that they just get mad when Lana gets nice.

"I'm going to make them see that I'm not their enemy. I want to be friends." She smiled wide and mockingly batted her eyelashes. "Don't worry so much Eliza! It's just Janice. Besides, she's going out with Jordan, that should preoccupy her and keep her mind off me."

Sunday, June 2nd, 1996

If someone asked me where Lana, my best friend, is, I'd honestly have to say, "I don't know." The last time I saw her was at school…three days ago. The police think she's run away. Lana has not run away, and I can't bring myself to tell them what has happened. I can't even bring myself to believe what has happened. I can't believe the truth.

—A sample of Holly's writing done outside of school

and confidence. Like Jamie, Holly wrote regularly outside of school. She said, "I probably write more out of school than in it." She kept all her writing in a box in her room. She regularly entered writing contests and had won a number of competitions. She has had her work published in several writing journals. She also wrote regular book reviews for the local newspaper.

Holly was aware of her own processes for writing and knew a variety of strategies to get started. "Reading and seeing how other authors write helps get me inspired, and so does turning on some music." She also talked about what helps her when she gets stuck: "It really helps to take a break sometimes." Like Jamie, she identified a particular time in her life when her interest in writing began—grade 1. She said, "In grade 1,

I had a teacher who taught writing and we did stories every week, and there were four or five other kids in the class who wrote a lot, too. We wrote so many stories back then. I think I still have them." Holly was also an avid reader with a large book collection, and recently read Susan Juby's, *Alice, I Think*, a clear favourite. She was also rereading Laurie Halse Anderson's *Speak*. Her two favourite genres for reading were realistic fiction and fantasy.

Holly pursued her interest in writing by attending Youth Write, a camp held during the summer months that put avid teenage writers together with experienced published writers. She said this experience helped her become a better writer and that she "learned that inspiration is everywhere, and you can get anything from anywhere to write about and to develop character." She said she learned at writing camp that teachers and writers are not synonymous and felt that published writers provide more realistic instruction than her teachers do. She also made a distinction between two groups of students at school—those who do writing assignments and those who are writers.

Matt

Matt was a tall, easygoing 14-year-old boy with a large smile and a quiet but confident manner. At the start of our first interview, Matt talked about a piece of writing he was working on, a lengthy story that was not quite a novel. He said that he had accessed a game website on the computer that has a link to writing, and there he was composing a story whose main character fit into the game. He admitted that he found this type of writing engaging and that he had been writing avidly since finding this website at the beginning of the school year.

Matt was aware of many processes he engaged in as a writer. He told me, for instance, that writing introductions was more difficult than writing bodies. His ideas came from a variety of sources, including songs, books, and movies. The website writing was very important to Matt: "I'll get my homework done and spend the whole night writing." Matt said that he preferred composing on the computer to writing longhand and that he was able to type much faster than he could write. For drafting, typing was much better for him than writing longhand. His parents figured into his life as a writer. Matt said that his parents "are really supportive. They've always encouraged me to write." Matt also acknowledged the importance of reading and watching television and movies to his writing. He said, "I think they [books] can be a big factor in why I write well."

Like Holly, Matt mentioned that he had had a positive experience as a writer in elementary school. He remembered writing a lengthy story— six pages—in grade 4 and reading it aloud to the rest of the class and that it received "a huge response." Matt also understood the importance of writing beyond drafting—that is, editing. And he talked about strategies that he used when he got stuck, such as rereading his work, taking time to think about his writing, and talking to others who might make suggestions to him. Matt said, "It's almost like a game sometimes.

Excerpt from "Thoressen"

Isyr sat in his tree, silent and unmoving. His red Dark Elf eyes stealthily kept watch over a lonely pass that wound through a nondescript mountain range. He had been tracking a renegade Khajit slave for the past week; he was expecting him to pass through any moment. At which point, Isyr would simply drop down on top of him, and after getting the better of him, send him back to his masters. The plan was simple enough, yet a staggering amount of preparation went into it; most of it making sure that he was invisible to the Khajit's naturally heightened sense of smell and equally powerful eyesight.

This particular plan of action had worked well for Isyr in the past, as he was more than capable of making himself blend in; a lifetime of bounty hunting had made Isyr quite competent at deception and trickery. However, for as good as he was, he was generally incapable of hiding himself from the magically inclined. His mother was something of an undiscovered magical powerhouse; had she not been born into slavery, she would have "made waves" as Isyr's brother, Sentri Thoressen, put it. There must have been some truth to that, as Isyr had heard rumours that Sentri had become a force to be reckoned with in recent years. Isyr had never cared for magic, for reasons he didn't fully admit to himself, but it had been proven that Isyr showed twice the raw aptitude for magic than Sentri ever had. For this reason, by simply existing, he unconsciously radiated a great deal of "magical disturbance" at random intervals. This meant that anybody who was searching for any magical disturbance would detect him without any trouble.

For everyone else, he was a ghost; a shadow. He had become a living legend to all manner of rogues and freelancers somewhere down the line, as stories about him got passed around taverns. As is the case with tales told over massive amounts of alcohol, details were eventually blown far out of proportion. The last time Isyr checked, he hailed from Oblivion, was nine feet tall, was capable of breaking boulders with his bare hands and could run faster than the wind. In reality, Isyr found himself to be a Dark Elf of moderate skills, lightweight build, and insignificant height. In essence, he wasn't the best at a lot of things, but he managed to get the job at hand done. Granted, his jobs tended to throw a lot of things his way that pushed him to his limits, but he scraped by, which was as much as any bounty hunter working in Morrowind could expect from life.

Thankfully, this job seemed to be running smoothly, even though it was an extremely long one. He was content to keep watching the path and surrounding foliage, watching for any movement whatsoever. After a few more minutes of this, Isyr was rewarded. His target, the scruffy, mangy Khajit runaway, came limping into sight, a large gash running the length of his leg. For a moment, Isyr couldn't understand how a smart, quick-witted Khajit could garner such a debilitating wound, until he heard the faint, distinct sound of Bonemold plates clicking against each other.

—A sample of fictional writing created by Matt outside of school

I'll get an idea from somebody else, and we'll hit it around a bit and I'll write about that." Like Jamie and Holly, Matt said he liked to read and especially liked books by Stephen King, *Dreamcatcher* being one of his favourites.

Their Guns Lay Silent

Whenever weather turns to frost,
We sadly remember the lives we lost.
Husbands, wives, they all are gone,
Even then, we must stay strong.
Women screaming, people crying,
These are the sounds of loved ones dying.
You rush to the door when it rings,
An officer with a flag, it's all he brings.
The feelings, the hurt, the hate inside,
The hate you feel for the other side.
But forgive them for mistakes they make,
Forgive them for the lives they take.
Their motives are hard to comprehend,
It seems so senseless in the end.
But, today we don't share their views,
We don't believe in hate or abuse.
Now the poppies lined in rows,
Take all our tears and all our woes.
So when a blossoming poppy is found,
It doesn't matter who's around,
Just say a prayer for those alive,
To help them deal with all those times,
Of losing friends, and seeing violence,
To let their thought stay in silence.
The eleventh is a frightful day,
It brought us pain in many ways.
A horrifying time for us all,
Not just another day in the fall.
Lest we forget on this morn,
That they are the reason our children are born.
Their guns stay silent, at peace they lay,
Upon this, our Remembrance Day.

—A poem written by Colin for a writing competition advertised in his English language-arts class at school

Colin

Colin was a very friendly, outgoing, and talkative grade-9 student at the first interview. When asked about his writing habits, Colin talked a great deal about two poems he had written for school and that were entered in writing contests. Colin said, "My poems are sad. I think the best poems are sad ones." Colin's teacher encouraged and praised his efforts in writing poetry, helping him to value his abilities as a writer. Colin said he did not do much writing apart from his school writing and responded to my question "Do you like to write?" by saying, "Yeah, I do. Surprising!"

Colin was most comfortable with the drafting stage of the process. He said of one of his poems in school, "I wrote half my poem in the first five minutes, it just all started coming to me." Colin was knowledgeable about planning strategies and mentioned brainstorming, freewriting, and webbing but preferred to draft his ideas without too much preplanning. Once the drafting was complete, or when he got stuck, Colin would seek the advice and help of others. He said he was comfortable asking the teacher and his peers for help. He named several students whom he approached to edit his work or confer with him when he was looking for assistance. Colin said, "There are so many good writers [in my class], and it's really easy to conference with them. They're all very good, and you can bounce stuff off them."

Colin credited a number of people with influencing his recent writing: an older brother, his teacher, other students, his grandparents, and his parents. His teacher taught him the mechanics of writing, like punctuation and grammar. However, he believed that improving the mechanics alone would not improve a piece of writing; he suggested, "It won't improve a writer's seriousness about a topic, it will just improve, you know, the basics." He also said that his teacher was helpful in giving input into his writing; it "gets my mind thinking again." He felt that his older brother was the "real" writer in the family and noted that his mom was also writing a book. When asked what he was particularly proud of, Colin spoke passionately about music: "Well, music is life." The relationship between writing and music was the source of his interest in writing. Colin said that he tried to read a lot and mentioned Matt Clancy as a favourite author.

Morgan

In the interviews, Morgan presented herself as a confident and relaxed 14-year-old. As we talked about writing, Morgan was quick to indicate that, while she was viewed as a good writer by others, it was not a label she completely identified with. On the other hand, she spoke enthusiastically about playing a variety of sports and was very proud of her membership on a representative soccer team. Morgan admitted that she liked to write but that her degree of enthusiasm really depended on the topic she was provided with. She said, "If it's not a good topic, I don't really try that hard." Morgan did say that she had done some writing on her own, outside of school and for her own purposes, when she was in elementary school. Interestingly, she thought she still had this early writing in a purple folder.

Morgan was aware of the processes she engaged in as a writer, particularly those of drafting, revising, and publishing. In school assignments, she drafted her ideas longhand and then used the computer for editing and typing out a clean copy. Her strengths were in spelling and at using vocabulary effectively. Morgan's ideas for writing often came from personal experience, and she started her writing by thinking about an experience and then changing it to create a new story. She preferred to write fiction and poetry. She shared two pieces of writing with me that she had written for school, one a poem and one a fictional letter written from the perspective of a soldier during World War II; she was pleased with these two pieces.

Morgan did not credit any other person with helping her or inspiring her to write; she viewed writing as mostly a solitary activity. She wrote

---

At the End of Every Rainbow

Hope
It used to seem so far away.
I was sad and lonely.
I felt like the world was on my shoulders.

My friends didn't understand,
That all I needed was a helping hand.
They were not my rays of hope.
And they were not the "pot of gold at the end of every rainbow."

I couldn't tell anyone how I felt.
I never even asked for help.
I was trapped in my own misery.
Holding a load that I couldn't carry.

Best friends long ago.
But then it hit me like a blow.
She stopped talking.
And kept walking.

Then I understood.
That I did all I could.
Apology letters, and endless sorrys.
It just wasn't enough.
I soon realized that I had to move on.

It took a long time.
I blamed myself for everything that I had done wrong.
And hated myself for the things that I couldn't do right.
I regretted my mistakes.
Even though I had no idea what they were.

But I was strong.
Learned how to cope.
I solved my problems.
I moved on.

—A poem written by Morgan for a school assignment

enthusiastically in her elementary-school years but was less enthusiastic in junior high. She recalled having written a lengthy piece in grade 4 or 5—approximately 30 pages long—and being proud of that. Morgan said that she read when she had the time and liked books by Mary Higgins Clarke.

Stephanie

Stephanie was a slight, quiet girl of 14 from a rural background. She attended a kindergarten-through-grade-9 school in a town of approximately 6000 people. Like the other students in the study, she was identified as a good writer by her grade-9 teacher. Like Morgan, Stephanie indicated that writing is an activity that she enjoyed if the topic was interesting. She said, "If you know what you are writing about, it all comes to you and everything, but if it's something that is new to you, then it's harder." She recalled writing a piece about babysitting, a topic with which she had

> **Remembrance Day**
>
> A day to remember
> A day to reflect
> On the loved ones we've lost
> As they tried to protect.
> As they fought all alone
>
> The crosses went up
> As the fighting went on
> The amputees left
> The rest were left as pawns
> And they fought all alone
>
> The families at home
> Would wait in suspense
> To hear of their fathers,
> Their husbands, their brothers
> They'd wait by the mailbox
> That was nailed to the fence
> To hear of the people who fought all alone
>
> Finally the day
> When they all would come home
> But one soldier says to you
> "I'm sorry . . ."
> And you're all alone

— A poem written by Stephanie for a school assignment

had a great deal of experience, and felt the writing she produced for that assignment was very good. When I asked her if she felt she was a good writer, she said, "Well, I'm pretty good. I get pretty good marks." She said she did a bit of writing outside of school but "not too much." She added, "Every once in a while, I'll write in my journal or just write poetry."

When we talked about the process of writing, Stephanie mentioned drafting, editing, and publishing. She said that her teacher suggested brainstorming and talking with others during the prewriting stage, but Stephanie did not think that these strategies were important. As did many of the other students, Stephanie did her drafting longhand and used the computer for editing, revising, and producing a clean copy. As did Matt, Stephanie talked about having had a positive audience reaction to her writing, which inspired her to continue. She talked about having written a piece about an imaginary first date and her friends saying, "That was so funny!"

Stephanie credited her grade-9 English teacher with inspiring her interest in writing. She said that she had even thought of becoming a junior-high English teacher herself. As did Morgan, Stephanie became animated when she talked about other activities she liked, particularly about her accomplishments in dance. When asked to consider if there were any similarities between writing and dance, Stephanie replied, "They both help me when I'm having a bad day. Take me away from my problems." Stephanie said she read when she had the time but did not mention favourites.

Micro-Organisms

By: Emma
File name: Science: Micro-organism poem

Whatever happened in 1674?
Anton van Leeuwenhoek walked through the door.

He discovered micro-organisms and a microscope,
The algae and fungi never had a hope.

There were protozoa, bacteria, and many tiny viruses,
In all different shapes and many different sizes.

One of the micro-organisms was shaped like a sphere,
This little thing triggered his career.

Algae is usually green, brown, or red,
They do not live alone but in colonies instead.

Bacteria are coloured blue and green,
On ponds these micro-organisms are usually seen.

Viruses are not alive or dead,
They are unknown by scientists that is what's said.

Then there is protozoa the biggest of them all,
They are bigger than bacteria, which is usually pretty small.

Last but not least, there are the fungi,
Mushrooms are a type that pop up and aren't shy.

Who would have thought that the scientist from the south,
Would have ever discovered micro-organisms in his mouth.

—A piece written by Emma for a school assignment

Emma

Emma was a friendly 14-year-old who attended a rural combination junior-senior high school with approximately 300 students. She was outgoing and talkative throughout the interviews. She said she liked writing and wrote both in school and on her own, though she said she had less time to write on her own as she got older. She distinguished between the two: "I think I can write more freely at home." Nonetheless, according to her teacher, Emma wrote well at school.

It was evident that Emma was knowledgeable about the process of writing. She credited her grade-8 English teacher with teaching her about planning, drafting, revising, editing, and publishing. She spoke about specific strategies that she used. For instance, she said, when she gets stuck, "I just go to a separate piece of paper and just write down a whole bunch of different ideas, then I can see if that will work if I put that into my writing." She spoke about ways she had been taught to revise and edit her work: "I read it out to myself, and then I usually give it to one of my friends, and they'll read it and then they'll help me if they see anything."

Emma pointed out that her teacher, too, was helpful by reading and editing her work. These comments indicated that Emma viewed the process of drafting and editing as separate processes. Emma used the computer infrequently in her writing because she preferred to write by hand: "I find it easier because I'll write it in one colour and then I can edit it in a different colour."

Emma did a lot of writing in elementary school. She credited her parents with showing her how to improve her writing, particularly with spelling, punctuation, and other mechanics of writing. Emma also credited her junior-high teacher with assigning different kinds of writing that were helpful and interesting. She especially appreciated learning how to write a business letter; one such letter was a complaint to a real company. Interestingly, when I asked her to talk about an accomplishment about which she was extremely proud, Emma talked about playing a variety of sports, basketball in particular. She was an avid reader and counted J.K. Rowling as one of her favourite authors. She was reading *Stargirl* by Jerry Spinelli at the time of the first interview.

Jaclyn

Jaclyn was a somewhat reserved but straightforward 14-year-old when I first met her. She spoke confidently about herself as a writer. She called herself "an aspiring writer." She lived on a farm and attended a rural combination elementary-junior high school with approximately 300 students. Later, she attended a high school in the same community. Jaclyn liked to read and write. She was eager to talk about specific writing she had done in the past and answered my questions fully and thoughtfully. Jaclyn had a preference for writing non-fiction, such as essays and research reports, although she was also drawn to poetry. She articulated the value of writing this way: "Writing has just always been there for me, ever since I've been little."

Jaclyn spoke confidently about the processes she engaged in when writing. As an example, she liked to brainstorm her ideas with her parents. She liked to draft in longhand but used the computer for final, clean copies, though she was not a very fast typist. She liked the "flowing" nature of writing longhand to the "chopping" nature of typing. For editing and revising, she liked her parents to help, even though there were opportunities in class for conferences with her teachers and peers. Jaclyn had a favourite place to write: at home on the roof.

Jaclyn said that her family was particularly supportive. Her parents looked at her work with a "semi-critical" eye, and she trusted their feedback. Like Holly, Jaclyn distinguished between those who were helpful and those who were not. She also talked about her grandfather, himself a cowboy-poet, and his influence on her writing. She said that her teacher, perhaps, did not agree with her about the direction her writing was taking and relied more upon the opinions of her parents. Jaclyn was an avid reader and said that Tolkein was one of her favourite authors. She was currently reading *The Day of the Jackal* by Frederick Forsyth.

Decisions of Conscience

Is right really that way, none can say,
Or is it wrong, just society's way.
The way of life never in rhythm,
Nobody's the same, that's why we're all different.

Society calls norm laws to norm.
Is that what shapes the right and wrong?
Or is it deeper than we can conceive,
Could it be morals, values, beliefs?

Morals differ with who we call sane.
Do morals not count while others remain?
Social rejects we presume to call,
Peoples whose lifestyles differ from ours.

Is there something deep in dept,
That we must call to or just go to wreck.
How can judges make a living of it,
Judging others but feeling no guilt.

We judge openly without thinking twice,
Talk first think last is our only device.
Do all our consciences work on the same tone,
Is it when we choose not to listen that shapes our choice.

Choice is of singular decision can be grouped,
Does that take all night round the loop.
Right in one aspect but not in the next.
Decisions of the present the end of the text.

—A poem written by Jaclyn outside of school

WHAT THE STUDENT PARTICIPANTS SAID

Question 1

My first question was: "What influences led to your interest in and aptitude for writing?"

Most of the student participants identified family members, friends, and specific teachers as influencing their development as writers. Trust was the most important thing. Two students believed that it was important to write for themselves as well as to seek an audience.

The role of audience has been discussed at length in the scholarly literature about writing. Some researchers suggest that, when one writes, it is mainly for self-expression and that self is the most important audience. Others suggest that writing is done mainly with an audience in mind. Jaclyn was one who believed in the importance of an audience: "Usually, in school, I get topics that I find are boring, and so I try and change them a little bit. I like writing about controversial things, because it gets a reaction. When I see the reaction in people it only influences my writing to be better."

Peter Elbow's experiences as a writer, teacher, and writing theorist indicate that both the self and an audience are necessary to a writer's development. The students who write mainly for themselves write outside of school as well as in school. Students who write mainly for an audience tend to write only when they are called upon to do so. As teachers, we need to seek out strategies that ask students to do both. We need to find ways to help students value their personal writing. Elbow phrases the dilemma this way:

> How can we conduct our teaching to maximize the opportunities for students to be good writers without experiencing themselves as "teacher pleasers?" Again, it is easy. We need new thinking and shrewd suggestions. (24)

Currently, writing instruction in middle- and high-school classrooms is failing our students, according to Elbow, because we are not doing enough to help them find their own purposes for writing. It is important to help students find their own purposes even when those purposes might conflict with ours, as teachers. Indeed, a good writing teacher could find him- or herself at odds with a student. The student's chosen topic might be undesirable or the form not acceptable, or we might not agree with the content. Even so, it is important that we help students understand that writing development is not only about pleasing the audience but also about helping them find out what it is that they want to say.

The students in my study thought reading had a significant influence on their topics and ideas for writing. They discussed how other forms of media, too, such as movies, computer programs and games, television, and radio affected their writing. Finally, they indicated that personal experiences and those of people they knew played a part in helping them decide what to write. Accordingly, teachers of writing need to do what Emma and Holly suggested: help teens be open to many different ideas.

It was interesting to discover how many of the participants had enjoyed very positive writing experiences in elementary school. Many of them identified a particular elementary teacher who encouraged them to write. Some even recalled a specific piece of writing that they had created, even its length and content. Most of the students had kept some of their earlier pieces.

The participants credited some of their teachers not just in the elementary grades but also in the middle- and high-school grades for contributing to their development as writers. In most cases, the teacher helped with the mechanics of their writing—spelling, punctuation, and vocabulary in particular. It is an inescapable reality for many middle- and high-school teachers that they often feel pressure to pay attention to the demands of standardized tests in writing, particularly in the area of writing mechanics. Since the demands of standardized testing have increased throughout North America over the past decade, high-stakes accountability is the norm in many states and provinces. Shelby Wolf and Kenneth Wolf, in their article entitled "Teaching True and to the Test in Writing," stress the importance of teachers responding to their students' writing and helping students reflect on their own writing, which in turn suggests the importance of encouraging students to write both for their own purposes and for an audience (229).

Question 2

The second question I asked was: Which instructional practices, in and out of school, have been helpful to you? Which practices have been unhelpful?

Several students talked about using the stages of The Writing Process, which had been presented in class. They used sophisticated writing terminology when discussing their own writing, which distinguished them as knowledgeable writers (see Swartzendruber-Putnam). All were able to identify strategies for prewriting, including webbing, brainstorming, conferencing with others, and making lists. The students were also able to talk about strategies they use when they get stuck. These included leaving the writing until another time, talking to others, changing the topic of the writing, and webbing.

The student participants all felt able to talk about the stages of The Writing Process and indicated that knowledge of it gave them independence when writing both in the classroom and at home. Three students said that knowledge about the process helped them get started on an assignment when others in the classroom appeared to be struggling. All the participants talked easily about various strategies within the process that they knew how to use. They noted that they needed to write in a number of classes (including English, social studies, and science) but felt that the various teachers were inconsistent in their methods of teaching writing. When asked if this was a hindrance, more than half of the participants said yes and that it would be helpful if their teachers all used the same terminology when talking about writing.

Many of the participants indicated that ideas usually developed quickly and that they appreciated knowing how to use the drafting stage to get the ideas down as quickly as possible. This is consistent with author Ray Bradbury's approach, in which he likens getting a writing idea to being bitten by a dog: it happens quickly and is often unexpected. Bradbury says that he completely gives himself over to the idea and writes until it is complete. Anne Lamott, in her book entitled *Bird by Bird*, says that, for her, an inspiration is "a kind of sweet panic growing lighter and quicker and quieter" (10).

While this type of instant inspiration sometimes could occur during school, for the participants such moments often came when they were at home. There, they said, they were not constrained by too much noise in the environment, for example, or at least they were in charge of the kind of noise they surrounded themselves with. Many preferred either a very quiet working environment or one with music that they liked. A few students said that they liked the school environment for writing because of the easy accessibility of the teacher and other students to help if they got stuck. But the majority preferred to write outside of school. They felt that they could move around more freely and that they could more easily control the noise. As well, they could write for as long or as short a time as they wanted.

The students gave fairly straightforward suggestions about how to design instructional strategies that encourage writers; however, they also talked about what I would term *ineffable* practices for encouraging writers. These ineffable practices challenge us as teachers to structure writing instruction in ways that are less straightforward. For instance, the students talked about needing to be open-minded in order to write; that is, be observant about what they see, hear, and read when deciding what to write about. They felt that a positive attitude was also important. Several participants talked about writing down their feelings as a way to get started. This is not unlike the advice provided by author Natalie Goldberg, who says that sometimes she begins by recording aspects of the present moment, like where she is sitting, what is on the table, what she is wearing, and what the weather is like (*Thunder* 23).

A few participants said they listened to or read about the views and habits of accomplished writers as a way to learn to write. One student, the one who had worked with experienced authors at a writing camp, suggested that the advice of experienced authors is helpful because "they are really writing all the time, and they know what you are going through." This particular idea speaks to an oft-made suggestion that teachers of writing must themselves be writers. There is considerable literature that encourages us, as teachers, to write on a regular basis and share our writing experiences with our students (e.g.: Atwell; Graves; Kittle). Most of these students did talk about some very specific strategies used by their teachers that they appreciated. These included the teachers' use of their own writing to teach editing skills, making transitions, and improving vocabulary and punctuation. Nearly every participant felt that a focus on interesting vocabulary was helpful.

Although the participants were hesitant to offer advice about unhelpful teaching practices, they were encouraged to do so as a way to help teachers improve writing instruction. The practice that students mentioned most frequently as unhelpful was the assignment of topics that they were either not interested in or knew nothing about. Some students said that, while teachers needed to provide specific topics from time to time to meet curriculum demands, it would be better to have some choice among a number of topics.

Most of the participants felt that time limits also inhibited them as writers and that, with a deadline, they often handed in writing that they did not like or that was not their best. One student commented, "It's frustrating when you are trying to learn about something, like from history, and suddenly the essay is due. It would be nice to have more time sometimes." However, most participants acknowledged that teachers needed to set a time limit for writing assignments during class time on occasion, but they did not want deadlines for all their writing.

The participants identified yet another unhelpful practice— assignments in forms that they did not like, such as the essay or poetry. There was much diversity among the participants about form. One student felt that essay writing was her forte, another preferred narratives, while another liked poetry. The students all developed their preferences early on in their lives. While they preferred opportunities to use their favourite forms, they saw the need to try others. Unfortunately, most of these students complained that teachers seemed to be looking for and rewarding formulaic writing that followed rules, which did not let the writer's voice come through. According to teacher and researcher Kathleen Andrasick, "formulaic student writing is due in part to a notion left over from the seventeenth and eighteenth centuries" (10) in which a single truth, often portrayed by teachers as a thesis statement, can be understood. This way of thinking has led in the past to teachers designing writing assignments that do not encourage creative or critical thinking. Andrasick says that it is time to move from writing that is too structured to writing that has limitless possibilities in terms of its forms, purposes, and audience. This is in keeping with research that shows that there are as many writing practices as there are writers. Even so, there are some common strategies that teachers can keep in mind when designing effective writing instruction. These include:

- teaching The Writing Process, which allows students to talk about their writing in terms of prewriting, drafting, revising, and publishing
- giving students choices of topics
- teaching a variety of forms
- focusing on aspects of writing that students themselves identify as important (e.g., vocabulary, punctuation, spelling, organization)
- providing a variety of environments for writing (e.g., quiet places, places with music, places where discussions can occur)

Question 3

The next question I asked the student writers was: What are your writing habits, both in and out of school?

The participants all spoke enthusiastically about their home environments for writing. Most wrote in their rooms at home, at a desk, or on the bed. They all talked about the need for quiet (or controlled noise) and solitude. One student said that her special place for writing was on the roof of her home, outside her bedroom. Some said that a quiet place for writing could sometimes be found at school but that the quiet seldom lasted for very long. Jamie said she wrote in her free time at home and noted, "I sometimes write for three hours a day when I get home. I write novels in my free time." One student said simply, "The classroom doesn't work for me." Another student said that writing in her room is motivating, because she can play the kind of music she likes and has the company of her cats. She said, "I like to have my cats around. They seem to be comforting. They are always there, and it's nice to have a little bit of company in the room when I write." These same students talked about being able have music playing in the background when they write. One said that certain kinds of music serve to inspire certain kinds of writing.

The teachers in my study, too, admit to frustration about the lack of solitude for students in the classroom; on drafting days, students often spend most of the period socializing (see Noskin). Nonetheless, writing in class allows teachers to monitor the process, provide assistance when necessary, and perhaps reduce the temptation for students to copy essays from the Internet. Finding appropriate environments at school, where classes have 25 to 35 students, can be be difficult. It can take some creative planning, including use of the library and the computer room, for example, to provide writing environments that work for all students.

The two participants who said that they wrote mainly at school did not feel that the school environment was unfavourable. Colin, for instance, spoke enthusiastically about a classroom environment that allowed for group work and a sharing aloud of ideas. He noted, "With student conferencing, you actually get to learn to work with others, and get their opinion, and see what other students are thinking." Colin was talking about what teacher and researcher Nancie Atwell refers to as peer conferencing—an interactive dialogue between writers. Peer conferencing can work in a classroom when students are ready and eager to participate in the revision and editing processes with others. However, for this to work successfully, most of the students need to be at the same stage of the process.

Jamie indicated that writing at school can be distracting: "When you're in the library, there are always people quietly talking or working on assignments, and it's confusing to try and work on your own writing." Another student said, "There are so many people making so many noises. The chairs aren't comfortable, the desk's not right, it's just not the right setting for me." The teachers in my study indicated that when the time was monitored well and students had a draft to work with, writing at school was worthwhile.

Even though all the participants had access to a computer in their own homes, most of them (all except two) said that they did most of their writing in longhand. This was somewhat surprising to us, given the push in schools to teach computer skills starting in elementary school. Only one participant said that he preferred the computer, and this was because he could not get his ideas down fast enough when he wrote longhand. Jaclyn said that she liked the way the writing "flowed" when she wrote longhand. Yet, all the students used the computer for creating a final, clean copy. One student said that she found it much easier to edit and revise when her work was on the computer. Some, once they had prepared their clean copies on the computer, regularly used the spell-check, grammar-check, and thesaurus features of the computer. Two of the participants indicated that the computer version of their writing looked better than a longhand version and made their writing more accessible to an audience, whether the audience was the teacher or other students.

Interestingly, as the participants moved from grade 9 to grade 12, most used the computer more and more frequently. They found that the speed with which they could work on the computer was important.

Question 4

The last question I asked the student participants was: What do you think is the value of writing?

Each participant valued something quite different about his or her ability to write, but all of them said that writing was important to them. This was perhaps not surprising, given that these students were considered by their teachers to be exemplary writers. Jamie, for instance, felt that writing filled a hole. She used it to examine things that were happening in her life and in the lives of others.

The students all spoke in a manner that showed care about their writing, and several indicated that they cared more when they wrote for a real purpose than when they did it just for a grade. Jaclyn described a writing assignment she did about a profession that bettered the world. She admitted that she liked to write about controversial issues and had chosen *mercenaries* as a topic. The teacher did not approve of the topic. Jaclyn, however, cared about the piece, partly, she admitted, for the effect it had on her teacher and her peers, and she worked hard on it anyway. Elbow writes that these kinds of struggles between teacher and student writer are necessary. Otherwise, "students may be paying too high a price in their compliance and preventing them from doing lasting good work" (25).

Providing students with real writing experiences for real audiences is important in helping students develop as writers. When the topic is right for a student, he or she seems to know it almost immediately and feels energized and excited about the topic. For example, Stephanie was excited to be able to write about her experiences when babysitting. Doing so allowed her to write humour and share it with others. Colin enjoyed writing song lyrics, which supported his interest in music.

Holly talked about writing just for the sake of writing. She viewed writing as an enjoyable, yet challenging, activity and one that she did regularly. She liked to write for an audience and often entered writing contests that provided feedback about the quality of the submissions. She credited her writing ability with having started at a very early age and having the support and encouragement of other people. Matt valued writing for the high self-esteem he felt. He was able to do all the writing assignments he received from teachers, which made him feel good, and he enjoying the writing he did on his own. He valued the fact that his writing was available to a wide audience on the Internet.

All the participants talked about the need for choice among topics and forms. They experienced a variety of writing assignments throughout their middle- and high-school years—poetry, essays, speeches, stories, editorials, letters, reviews, and debates—and they expressed their preferences for certain forms and topics. Matt, for instance, suggested that he could write about the topic provided for him by the teacher but found essays far more difficult than stories. Emma remembered being asked to write a report on the environment but was given the opportunity to choose a specific animal to research and write about.

All the student participants mentioned assignments that offered little or no choice of topic or form and said that the restriction affected their ability to write well. They were aware that their teachers had a curriculum to cover and acknowledged this before saying, for example, "But if I could have some choices about what I write about, I'd do a better job on my writing." One student remembered being assigned a movie review and said that every student in the class wrote about the same movie. She wondered why students could not choose their own movies (within reason). The partcipants did understand that it was the job of their teachers to teach them to write in a variety of forms (e.g., essays, letters, reviews, poetry, and stories). However, within those forms, they would like to have been allowed to make choices about the topic.

Several of the participants talked about the value of writing to express feelings. Jamie and Emma, for example, discussed writing as a creative outlet. Jamie said, "Writing kind of helps me get everything out, like if I feel depressed. If I write then, it helps me to get it out and I'll feel better. It just seems like a part of my heart when I write, because I put my heart into it all the time." Jaclyn said that without writing in her life, she would probably be a lot angrier. "That's how I vent—in my writing. And I have no other way to do that constructively. Well, recently I've begun to play hockey, but I never used to have that." Holly wrote in a journal on a regular basis, as did Jamie; they wrote for self-expression and for their own purposes.

When working on a school assignment that required students to write poetry, Colin wrote about Remembrance Day in a poem he entitled "Their Guns Lay Silent." Colin said that this piece was emotional and heartfelt.

When students are helped to find the topics that matter to them and the forms that best fit those topics, they are able to use writing as a "way to show their knowledge, their questions, their opinions, their fears, their dreams, their imaginations" (Rief 59).

The Writers Workshop

Beginning a writing workshop can be a lot of fun. For once you won't have to generate all the content and struggle to teach it to passive learners. The writing workshop puts students on the spot and requires them to be active learners. If it's done right, your students' inexhaustible energy—their stories, interests, passions will fuel the learning environment. (Fletcher and Portalupi 37)

Goal of this Chapter

My goal in this chapter is to show how one of the strategies for teaching writing, the writers workshop, can help students develop their writing skills. I present the workshop that was part of my study entitled "Learning about Writing Instruction: What Teens Tell Us." The workshop was presented in five stages, which correspond in a general way to The Writing Process.

In the spring of the students' grade-9 school year, we organized a writers workshop so that the participants of my study ("Learning about Writing Instruction: What Teens Tell Us") and their teachers could work with a published author. The study began in the fall, so, by the spring, I knew the students well and had interviewed each of them once. We were fortunate in being able to engage Canadian writer Linda Holeman, who had at that time already published several children's and young-adults' books.

THE WORKSHOP IN FIVE STAGES

Stage 1: Getting Started

The participants and their teachers arrived at the University of Lethbridge early in the morning on the day of the workshop. We settled into a brightly lit, small-sized classroom with large glass windows that looked out onto the Education Library. The room contained several trapezoidal tables organized into two horseshoe shapes. The students sat in the horseshoe closest to the front, and Linda sat in the middle.

The teachers and I sat behind the students in the other horseshoe. Linda greeted the students as they came into the classroom; most of them seemed a bit nervous and tentative. After some informal conversation and greetings, the students and the teachers introduced themselves to the group, and Linda began the workshop.

Linda quickly acknowledged that writing in a workshop situation for the first time can be a bit intimidating and assured the students (and us teachers) that no one could be "wrong" in this setting—whether speaking or writing. She also pointed out that one of the ways to be helpful to a writer was to avoid criticizing. However, saying something like "I don't understand what that means" about a piece of writing was appropriate.

She said that many people dream about being writers. They often say, "When I retire, I will be able to do some writing," but, for many people, the time never comes when they do that. She asked us what we thought about that. Several students felt that if you wanted to be a writer, you would make the time to do it, no matter what. Some said that sometimes you do not have control over the writing that you do. It just comes. Linda agreed and added, "There are things, characteristics, that make us writers. What do you think those characteristics are?" The students identified some of the characteristics that distinguish them from their classmates: needing and liking to be alone sometimes; liking to watch and observe people and situations; being sensitive to their surroundings; being able to see things that other people do not. Linda said that these were characteristics that she would use to describe herself.

Linda said that freewriting as a first step has been helpful to her. Peter Elbow says that freewriting "frees the writer from planning, from meeting the needs of readers, and from any requirements as to what [the writer] should write about or how [the writer's] writing should end up" (383). Linda found this a good way to begin her writing, even though the freewriting work might not necessarily translate into a publishable text.

Stage 2: Drafting

Linda insisted that it is necessary for a writer to regularly engage in practice writing, which sounded very much like writer Natalie Goldberg's approach: "In the beginning, I wrote for rounds of ten minutes, eventually increasing them to twenty and thirty. I kept my hand consistently moving for the full time" (*Thunder* 15). Linda asked us to think of a smell and suggested that we do the following quick exercise:

The smell of _____.

always makes me think of _____.

She asked us to write non-stop for five minutes and added, "Be in touch with not only the good things you think of but also the bad ones." Everyone wrote: students, teachers, and Linda herself. Matt's piece went like this:

> The smell of new cars always makes me think of, well...new cars. This smell stands out from the rest because it's the only smell that can really make me feel ill. I came across this unpleasant fact yesterday when I spent nearly four hours in my sister's new car.

Holly wrote:

> The smell of hotdogs always makes me think of the fairgrounds. Smells mixing together from over-worked machinery. Smelling of green, black and orange.

Jaclyn's written text was:

> The smell of freshly made ice from a hockey rink reminds me of a special friend I lost prematurely. Her smiling face, her sweet laugh. To know that never again would I speak to her or laugh at her corny jokes.

Following this quick exercise, Linda said that some writers have certain themes that define their work. She said that much of her writing deals with longing and searching for home and uses experiences from her childhood. She also said that there are many places where writers can search for ideas, particularly by observing themselves and those around them, and by noticing what is happening among these people. She encouraged us to remember our dreams (both sleeping and waking) for ideas. She suggested that teens keep a writers notebook with them at all times, helpful because thoughts that come quickly can disappear just as quickly if not recorded.

Linda then asked the participants what they needed to have in their lives in order to write. Their responses included the need for silence, rhythm, and boredom. This indicated to me and the teachers the importance of providing a classroom environment that encourages writing.

Then it was time for another writing exercise. This time we were asked to think of a character—someone our own age, either male or female—peering into a refrigerator. We were asked to write about a conflict facing this person. As with the first writing exercise, the students began writing immediately and did not stop until Linda asked them to do so. Emma wrote:

> "Where's my science project? I put it in the fridge," yelled Jared.
> "Dad," he called again, "have you seen it?"
>   "Seen what, son?"
>   "My science project," he replied, very annoyed.
>   "What does it look like?" his father asked.
>   "It's a bowl of Jell-o mixture with green stuff on top," Jared answered.
>   "Was it in the blue and red bowl?" his father asked.
>   "Yes, it was. Do you know where it is?" Jared asked again.
>   "Uh-oh," his father said, "it was very tasty."

Matt wrote:

> If I wasn't sure before, I definitely was now. The fridge had stopped working the day before and, opening the door carefully, I almost passed out from the smell of rotting vegetables and

fruit. Muttering curses under my breath, I kicked the six-foot box several times in frustration, then picked up the phone and called Jim. I dialed it twice before I got it right. After a brief conversation, I finally convinced Jim to come over and take a look.

Morgan wrote:

As she opened the fridge door, Dominique smelled something awful. Bent over, peering deep inside the fridge, she tried to figure out what the foul smell was and where it was coming from. She followed her nose, pushing it in every direction. Then she came across an ugly green and mouldy blob sitting on a plate near the back of the fridge. Plugging her nose, she took it out and hurled it into the garbage. What was it? She'll never know.

Jamie wrote:

What was it you wanted?" Linda called from her stooped position within the fridge opening.

"Water," a small voice replied from the tiny living room.

Linda glanced into the fridge again, pushing aside cartons and cold items. Where was the jug?

"You can get it from the tap if you want," called the voice.

"No, here it is." Linda grabbed the jug of water from the corner of the fridge.

Jaclyn first wrote: "I draw a blank." Then she wrote:

As if by instinct, he enters the house, drops his bag on the chair, which is placed strategically by the door, and goes to the fridge. Upon opening it, he sees a perfectly wrapped envelope addressed to him. It puzzles him. He stands for a moment as if in awe of such a simple thing. Standing with a stricken look on his face, fridge door open, gazing at it in a stupor, he finally opens it.

It was interesting to note how differently each student interpreted the writing exercise. Each writer used his or her own personal experience and background, coupled with an idea, to create a piece of writing. Linda pointed out that no interpretation had been wrong. Rather, they had created text that could be left as is or turned into something different later on.

Stage 3: Sharing the Writing

Even though the teens were just getting to know one another in the workshop, Linda talked to them about the importance of reading their writing aloud. According to Nancie Atwell, teens need the chance to share their writing with others—peers, teachers, parents, for example—and with themselves. They need to hear their writing and decide what to do next with it.

Linda asked the students if they would be comfortable reading aloud what they had written. They nodded, and Matt began. The students responded positively to one another's work, which made for a relaxed environment, and Linda gave them lots of positive comments. Then she asked the participants to notice specific aspects about one another's writing and to comment on them. They noticed the dialogue, the sense of mystery, the humour, and the characters.

Next, Linda invited the students to ask her questions. Several wanted to learn about the publishing process, asking about how it works and about how to deal with rejection letters. Linda admitted freely that rejection always feels bad, but because rejection letters usually focused on the negative, they could be used as important feedback for improving one's writing. The students also asked about her own experience with problems such as writer's block. Her advice was to keep writing and to give herself permission to write badly for a while. She helped the students understand that sometimes a writer loses faith in him- or herself and stressed that this is something every writer faces. The students were surprised to hear Linda say that she thought she would never tackle writing a novel and had started out with short stories. They were also surprised to hear her say that even experienced writers suffer from self-doubt. (She said that she eventually did write a novel.)

Then, for the final writing exercise, Linda had the students each select a topic from a hat: bats, umbrellas, babies, roses, cashews, Santa, candles, crosses, rain, and mosquitoes. She observed how quickly these students began writing and how she hoped that, if they were this eager in school, their eagerness was rewarded. Stephanie wrote:

> As the rain comes pouring down, I get this urge to run outside and feel and smell its freshness. It's cold outside. Once the rain has stopped, the sun comes out and begins to dry everything around me.

Holly wrote:

> I am smelling cashews and thinking of the hospital. I am allergic to nuts and try to stay away from them. Only, one day, I mistook a cashew for a sunflower seed and had to be rushed to the hospital. I could feel my throat closing up as we raced across the Westside Bridge to get there.

Colin wrote about mosquitoes:

> To the pests. The thought of thousands of mosquitoes swarming around me scares me to the depths of my soul. It is amazing how a bug so tiny can bring about so much anger. I doubt that anyone anywhere likes mosquitoes. An undying stream of buzzing, itching and flying. Those tiny little devils in the sky.

Morgan wrote about crosses:

> I visit the crosses almost every day. There are so many rows. Crosses all around. It's sad to see how so many have died, with the cross being all that we have to remember them by. Full of pain and loss of a loved one, the cross is put into the ground. Another life lost. Another time to mourn.

Jaclyn wrote:

> Candles. Flicker, flicker...stop...flicker. Still alive in the lightest sense of the word. The candle, the single solitary candle, alone in the hall. The wax slowly softens and melts, falling down the steep sides like a mudslide. Slowed down just enough to witness the marring left by that which preceded it before devouring the sides. In its own unique patterns before finally meeting its shy end.

Jamie wrote:

> I walk through the brightly lit mall, anticipating, searching for the one I am to meet. My mother's soft hand holds on to me as she leads me through the crowd. I am surrounded by other children of all ages. Finally my eyes land on a golden throne as the crowd slowly begins to move back. And there, sitting on the throne, in a red velvet suit and with bushy silver hair, rosy cheeks and a joyful laugh, sits Santa Claus. It is my turn to make a Christmas wish.

Emma wrote about babies:

> The first cry of a newborn tells us that a new life has entered the world. The eyes, trying to make sense of us. Helpless but loved like nothing else on earth. Tiny hands that fit around your thumb as you hold them close to your heart. Unaware of what is going on around them. They are babies, beautiful new human beings.

Matt wrote about bats:

> The bats I grew up with could never be considered normal bats. They never waited for the night, allowing them the cover of darkness. They could usually be seen in the failing light, hunting with machine-like precision for their prey. Their prey wasn't normal either. Pieces of candy left on the ground or an open trashcan that had toppled over spilling its contents everywhere. They weren't powerful or terrible. No, they looked more like some sort of deranged flying rat, with undersized wings and fat bodies.

Stage 4: Finishing Up

Linda had the participants share their writing once again, and she observed aloud that they wrote with enthusiasm and thoughtfulness—two important attributes of good writers. She pointed out how each was beginning to develop an individual style but added that it can be helpful to try other writers' styles. She finished the workshop by thanking the students and their teachers for participating so eagerly. Finally, she advised them not to throw any of their writing out: "Keep all your work, because it is interesting to see how your writing changes over time, and you never know when you'll need a piece to work into a story you are working on."

Stage 5: Getting Feedback from the Participants

In the second interview that I conducted with each participant, I asked them to talk about how the workshop had benefited them as writers. I also asked them to compare the type of instruction they received in the workshop with that of their English language-arts classrooms.

All the students said that they appreciated the opportunity to work with a "real," published author. Jaclyn said, "It was really useful listening to an author, someone who writes full-time as a profession. To be able to see how she wrote and what worked for her." Others agreed, indicating that meeting and talking to an author helped them see where their own writing could lead.

Five of the students said that they appreciated Linda's comment that writers need to be sensitive observers of people, their surroundings, and their interactions. Jamie identified with Linda's comment that writers tend to like to be alone: "Well, when Linda said that writers tend to be kind of quiet and that they like sticking to themselves, and that is like me." Matt also thought Linda's comment was interesting; he said, somewhat jokingly, "I guess I thought of myself when she said writers tend to be sensitive because people are always saying to me, 'You're so sensitive,' and you know that can be either a good thing or a bad thing, but she made it seem like it was a good thing." Holly said that it was nice to have time to herself to write but that it was possible to write with others around if they are trustworthy. She referred particularly to her experience at a writing camp, where students listened to drumming for inspiration. She observed, "When we listened to the music, we talked about a character that we created and then we pretended to be that character, and that really helped the writing about him or her." She related this experience to Linda's observations about what writers tend to do. Jaclyn added, "One of the things Linda said was that silence and being alone really works, and I really connected with that."

As might be expected, the students enjoyed learning about the publication process from someone who has experienced it. They were surprised to find out how long the entire process takes and found it interesting that some authors work with agents and others do not. Stephanie commented that the publishing information was interesting but that she did not think she would take steps in the near future to have any of her writing published.

Also interesting to the participants was the opportunity to listen to one another in the presence of an author. Colin pointed out, "I thought the workshop was too short, because I was enjoying listening to everyone's writing. It made me want to write more." Jamie agreed: "At first I was nervous about sharing my writing with someone I didn't know very well. But I got used to it near the end of the workshop."

Finally, all the students said that the writing exercises had been fun and beneficial to them. Morgan said that the "hands-on" aspect of the workshop was helpful to her. Others noted that the exercises challenged them to write about topics they would not otherwise consider, and they found that interesting. One student thought that another author would likely have had them write about different topics, and said that it would therefore be beneficial to work with other authors. It was interesting to note that every student in this group began writing almost immediately after a topic was suggested and did not stop easily. Linda confided to the teachers and to me that she found this refreshing. When asked how the workshop differed from the type of instruction they received in their classrooms, most students said that their classroom teachers focused on the basics of writing. Jamie said that she had learned in class about various forms—including essays, poetry, and stories—and that her teacher was most helpful with the aspect of vocabulary. She said, "She [the teacher] helps me use special words, different ones that I haven't used much that will have an impact in my story." This experience was echoed by most of the other students; their classroom teachers helped them mainly with punctuation, sentence structure, transitions, vocabulary, and organization. While a few students said that worksheets helped them learn these skills, most indicated that they learned them at the draft stage without the help of aids. Most of the participants felt that they were already good at spelling but wanted to improve their vocabulary.

Holly commented that her teacher assisted her with some of the technical skills of writing, but she also noted, "I'm not sure if you can teach writing. Maybe you can't do it. The writer has to sort of have an idea and be able to put all the ideas and emotions on paper. You can't teach something that is in your head, because it has to come from the student." Jamie and Colin agreed and said that their writing was best when it was heartfelt. Once they had been able to draft something emotionally meaningful, they could then work on various other aspects of their writing to improve it, such as vocabulary, spelling, and punctuation.

Overall, the participants experienced this workshop as a type of "think-tank." It was a place to practice writing fluency without the pressure of having to progress to a final copy or to publication.

WHAT THE WRITERS WORKSHOP TAUGHT US

The writers workshop was a highlight of these students' writing lives to that point, which indicated to us that effective teaching in secondary schools needs to include workshop experiences. The participants and their teachers saw the benefit of five specific conditions under which students may improve their writing. These include: (1) knowledge of The Writing Process, (2) time for extended writing practice, (3) access to writing professionals, (4) knowledge of revision and editing techniques, and (5) prompt evaluation. (See figure 3.1.)

Knowledge of The Writing Process

One of the most important differences between the participants in the workshop and their peers, according to their teachers, is that the participants were knowledgeable about The Writing Process and about their own personal approaches to writing. Given the vast literature on The Writing Process over the past 20 years, it is reasonable to say that we need to teach The Writing Process in our schools. But we conclude from our study that instruction must go further than just teaching The Writing Process. We need to make students aware of the difficulties and challenges they might face as writers. We also need to give them the strategies that they can use when their writing seems difficult, if not impossible, to do.

Time for Extended Writing Practice

The teens in our study all spoke about the benefits of writing on a regular basis, both in structured situations such as writers workshops and school, and in their own time. Many of them said that they wrote at home, for

- Provide frequent and uninterrupted time for writing, either on a daily or a weekly basis.

- Have students talk about or write about their thoughts and feelings about writing on a regular basis.

- Write on a regular basis yourself. Share your thoughts and feelings as a writer.

- Provide a variety of purposes, audiences, and forms of writing for your students. Ask students to talk about their preferences for each.

- Group students according to their preferred working environment; those who like quiet can work together, those who like similar music can work together, and those who need opportunities to talk about their ideas with others can work together.

- Demonstrate revision and editing strategies to students.

- Help students link personal writing to expository pieces.

- Evaluate students' writing by talking to them about criteria, grading, and feedback.

Figure 3.1. A summary of effective teaching strategies for writing instruction in secondary schools

their own purposes. The teacher participants said that they could always tell which of their students wrote at home and which students wrote only at school.

Access to Writing Professionals

The participants—students and teachers alike—all felt that it was helpful for beginning writers to understand how published writers work and think. Workshops and less formal presentations in school by experienced writers are very helpful. The teacher participants noted, however, that they, themselves, can do more to become experienced writers. The teacher-as-writer approach to instruction could be even more helpful. Penny Kittle, in her article entitled "Writing Giants, Columbine, and the Queen of Route 16," says, "[Before I began writing with and for my students], I simply didn't know what I was asking my students to do. Now I write regularly with my classes. I attempt to craft the writing I assign and share my frustrations and my failures, my eurekas and my successes, with my students" (11).

Knowledge of Revision and Editing Techniques

The participants felt that they benefited from their teachers' instruction in revising and editing. While not every student felt that the manner in which the instruction provided by their teachers in revising and editing was helpful, they did understand how important it can be. Revision was perceived by some students as pertaining only to spelling, punctuation, and grammar. However, others understood revision as a more elaborate process—finding the exact word to convey meaning and bouncing ideas off others, for example. Shanahan suggests that this fuller type of revision "may include both highly formal and elaborate approaches to making changes in a manuscript, or it can involve much less formal discussions of the ideas that were included in the students' papers without actual rewriting"(68). Students need to see teachers model this type of activity if they are to engage in it themselves.

Prompt Evaluation

The participants talked about the importance of receiving prompt feedback. The teachers agreed, but they also said that they sometimes felt overwhelmed by the sheer quantity of the writing that they had to mark. This was especially true when they were teaching several English and/or social studies classes at a time. In many provinces and states, there is considerable pressure to grade all student writing according to standardized test rubrics. Students become familiar with the rubrics and then adjust their writing to meet the expectations of the achievement tests. But rubrics have been coming under increasing scrutiny lately (see Narter). For English teachers, rubrics are often an unsatisfactory tool for measuring the tone and stylistic peculiarities that distinguish good writing from mediocre, yet correct, writing. Teacher and writer David Narter's answer to this challenge is to treat each writer as an individual. In his article entitled "Teacher as Machine," he writes, "The teacher must respond to the student's work as an individual reader critically engaging in the work of a writer" (67). (For a full discussion of rubrics for assessing and evaluating writing, see chapter 5.)

Using The Writing Process

A friend of mine says that the first draft is the down draft—you just get it down. The second draft is the up draft—you first fix it up. You try to say what you have to say more accurately. And the third is the dental draft, where you check every tooth, to see if it's loose or cramped or decayed, or even, God help us, healthy. (Lamott 26)

Goal of this Chapter

My goal in this chapter is to provide practical and concrete ways to teach writing in secondary schools. I offer research-based and teacher-tried strategies that correspond to each of the five stages of The Writing Process.

At some point, as teachers of various subjects, we give writing assignments to students. For example, science teachers ask students to write lab notes, social studies teachers assign essays and editorials, drama teachers have students write scripts, and teachers of other disciplines ask students to keep learning logs, write in journals, and take notes. The degree to which we teach students how to write depends on our own experiences as writers, our educational backgrounds, our individual interests, and our confidence about teaching writing. Yet, secondary-school teachers often lament the fact that students do not write well. One high-school teacher describes his students' writing in this way:

> And their papers were all bad. Oh, they were mechanically fine. Beginnings, middles, and ends. Decent spelling. No big usage problems. But they were dull. Ordinary. Not a fresh thought in the group. It was like reading cold mashed potatoes—the instant ones. Blah. (Andrasick 4)

This type of response often occurs when students do not have a personal connection to what they are writing, nor do they have the strategies to produce a thoughtful, organized, creative, and critical piece of writing. Many teachers themselves do not know the principles of The Writing Process. We urge all teachers, not just those who teach language arts, to familiarize themselves with it and begin using it. Teachers will almost certainly notice that students are starting to write more effectively.

The Writing Process is invaluable in teaching writing to teens. It identifies the stages that writers go through, which helps students and teachers see where there are problems. The process provides students with a place to start, or start again, when they get stuck. It is important that the process not be used in a formulaic way—that is, when students use the stages mechanically and without critical thought. Rather, it should be used to provide students with many varied opportunities to write. For example, the process can help students come up with topics for writing, know what to do when they are stuck, or use writing to evaluate, analyze, and compare ideas.

PREWRITING

Prewriting is the stage when writers consider what to write about. The teacher sometimes sets the writing task. Other times, the teacher provides ideas for students to choose from, and, still other times, the teacher asks students to write on self-selected topics. No writer approaches prewriting in the same way. While it is helpful to give all students opportunities to prewrite, teachers should not insist that all students do this, especially when the activity leaves them unmotivated or unable to write. Some students, including several I worked with throughout my study on teen writers, indicate that they prefer to begin writing as quickly as possible (skip to the drafting stage) and figure out where their writing will take them as it happens.

Brainstorming

Perhaps one of the best ways to begin The Writing Process (in prewriting) is brainstorming. This is a strategy involving drawing circles and filling them in with words that describe ideas (brainstorming maps) or making lists with interconnecting lines (brainstorming plans). There is no one right way to brainstorm, but it can be helpful for the teacher or a peer to talk with the students during the process. The resulting pages can later be used as a word bank for the piece. (See appendix A and figure 4.1.)

The K-W-L Chart

A K-W-L chart can be a great way for students to begin researching a topic. Researcher Donna Ogle introduced K-W-L charts as a way to help students organize their thoughts during content learning, and it is valuable in a variety of subject areas. Students, whether working in collaborative groups among themselves or with the teacher, start by developing a list of information that they already know (K) about their chosen topic. Once students have researched the topic (K and W) and recorded it, they go back to the K-W-L chart and record what they have learned (L) about their hero.

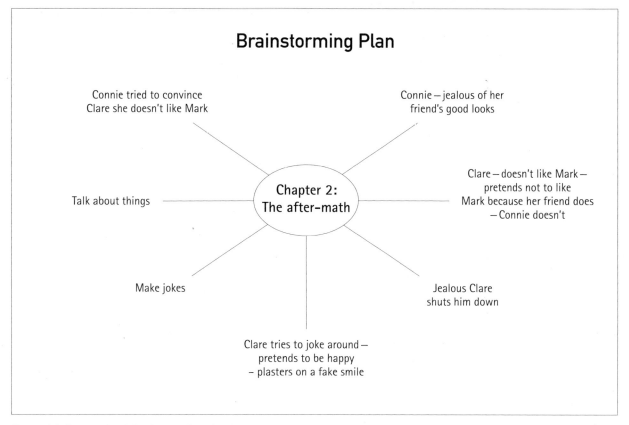

Figure 4.1. One student's brainstorming plan for getting from the first to the second chapter of a story

A modified K-W-L chart has an additional column (S), where students record what they still want to learn (S). It is important to notice that, when the students are filling in the S column, they are engaging in metacognition (thinking about thinking); they are reflecting on what has been learned throughout the research process. They are evaluating the resources, the information, and the final report. Andrasick calls the still-want-to-learn phase "looking, distancing, manipulating" (58) and believes that it gives students greater control over their writing. (See appendix B.)

See figure 4.2, which shows how a group of students used a K-W-L-S chart to organize their study of a favourite hero—Mahatma Gandhi.

Outlining

Outlining is another strategy for helping students get their writing started. It can be helpful to those students who do not want to begin writing until they know where the writing is going. As well, it is helpful to do an outline during writing. I encourage students to develop a sequential set of topics and sub-topics that represent the main ideas, which they then use as a structure. Some teachers consider outlining to be too formal a way to begin writing. Many students who are asked to use outlines find it much easier to produce one only after the writing has been done. (See figures 4.3. and 4.4.)

K-W-L-S Chart

Topic: Mahatma Gandhi

K	W	L	S
What do I know?	**What do I want to know?**	**What have I learned?**	**What do I still want to know?**
• Gandhi was a leader in India.	• When did he live? Where was he educated?	• Gandhi lived from 1869 to 1948.	• How did Gandhi use non-violent action?
• He was known as someone who sought peaceful means in seeking change.	• What did he do for a living?	• He was educated as a lawyer in London and worked for a time in South Africa.	• What kind of lifestyle did Gandhi follow?
• He portrayed a calm, passive approach.	• What was he fighting for?	• He fought for India's independence from Great Britain.	• Did I find the kind of information I was looking for?
• He is known as someone who used fasting as a form of protest.	• What were other means he used to seek change for India?	• He, himself, experienced racial discrimination.	• Did I use web resources and book resources?
	• What is his greatest legacy?	• He believed in non-violent action to resist British rule.	• Which were the most helpful?
		• In 1929, he led 50 000 people on a 320-km march to the sea.	• Is the report written in my own words?
		• His life was characterized by simplicity and harsh self-discipline.	

Figure 4.2. K-W-L-S chart created by a student studying Mahatma Gandhi

I.

   A.

   B.

     1.

     2.

       a.

       b.

         i.

         ii.

   C.

Figure 4.3. A template for prewriting or monitoring

Dead Poet's Society Outline

I. Introduction

Thesis Statement: In Peter Weir's film, *Dead Poet's Society*, Mr. Keating was an example, and clearly showed Neil, Todd, and Charlie how to embrace the theme of individualism.

- ever been afraid to stand out?
- do something even if no one else is doing it?
- take a stand for something you believe in?

II. Body Paragraph #1

Thesis Statement: Neil was an individual in all senses.

- started Dead Poet's Society
- tried out for the play
- recognizes his dreams, and goes for them
- reaches out to other guys who aren't as confident (Todd)

III. Body Paragraph #2

Thesis Statement: Todd Anderson truly displayed an individual attitude.

- said he wouldn't read even when everyone else did
- everyone expected him to be like his brother, but he didn't try to be just like him
- wanted to stand up for Mr. Keating even when none of the other guys did
- stood on his desk and said, "Oh Captain, my captain"

Use these ideas as examples in other paragraphs:

- Mr. Keating showed his students what it is to be an individual.
- Mr. Keating had a different teaching style even when the students weren't expecting it and when it wasn't accepted at Wellton.
- Mr. Keating showed the guys how to think for themselves.

IV. Body Paragraph #3

Thesis Statement: Charlie Dalton was confident in himself, which helped him to truly be an individual.

- changed his name to Newanda
- "phone call from God"
- published the letter
- exercised his right not to walk
- brought girls to Dead Poet's Society
- painted his chest

V. Conclusion

Through Mr. Keating in *Dead Poet's Society*, the characters of Neil, Todd, and Charlie learned how to deny conformity. Individuality, individual character—the sum of the qualities that make one person or thing different from another. Conformity—behaviour in agreement with generally accepted standards of business, law, conduct, and worship and fitting oneself and one's thoughts to the ideas of others; compliance.

Figure 4.4. An outline created by a student for an essay on the main ideas in the movie *Dead Poet's Society*

Prewriting Conferences

To help them think about topics for writing, it is useful for teachers to engage students in conversations either alone or with several other students. The idea of talking about thoughts and ideas before putting them on paper is a well-established strategy used by elementary and middle-school writing teachers (Atwell). It is based on the theoretical work of Lev Vygotsky, who points out, "Thought is not merely expressed in words; it comes into existence through them" (218). Many students who are reluctant writers have well-developed oral skills that they can use for writing. A small-group conference is an excellent forum for establishing suitable topics, helping the writer get started, and even assisting the writer identify audience, purpose, and format. Talking prior to writing can be a significant motivator for students. It can often provide them with the confidence to begin writing.

Teachers can assume either a passive or an active role during a conference. Some students need to reassure themselves that they have something to write about. They can do this by talking about their ideas and having those ideas acknowledged and accepted. Here, the teacher acts passively. Other students may need the teacher to take an active approach, more direction, which can come about during the conference through careful questioning by the teacher. The teacher might guide the student toward a topic and suggest an audience and format. Some suggested conference questions are:

- Can you tell me what you are interested in—hobbies, activities, friends, places?
- What do you already know about this topic?
- Do you need to find additional information in order to get started on this topic?
- Where can you find the information that you need?
- What are you writing this piece for? To inform? To entertain? To convince? To argue? To describe?
- Are you writing this piece as yourself? As someone else?
- What form will your writing take? A letter? A journal entry? An essay? A review? A news story? An editorial? A critique? A cartoon? A lab?

Writers Notebook

Many teachers encourage students to keep a writers notebook, which they carry with them throughout the day. They could use it to list the topics and areas of interest that might be written about at some later date. They might use it to record ideas, snippets of conversation, observations about their surroundings, and what people around them are doing. They might paste in newspaper or magazine articles. Teachers can nudge their students into using their notebooks by saying something like, "Now, that was interesting. Perhaps you could put it in your notebook and write about that sometime." Then, when students get into the habit of observing their surroundings on their own, they begin to realize that inspiration for writing can come from anywhere. They learn that their own lives and imaginations provide the stimulus for writing, which can be a tremendous boost to the student's confidence as a writer. Carrie Netzel, one of the

To me, a door is very symbolic. When a door is closed, that means that we do not know what is behind it. We do not know what the next stage in our life will hold for us, if it will be good or bad. We know that we have the power to open the door, the power to twist the knob and expose what is on the other side. I do not know whether the key is going to unlock the door or whether it is locking the door. If it were locking the door, it could symbolize that that stage of our life is over, in our past. It could also mean that we are protecting secrets on the other side, secrets that we do not want to share with anyone else. If the key is going to unlock the door, it could mean that we are now ready to move on to the next stage of our life. However, it is not there yet. This could symbolize our uncertainty, our fear and our confusion about life. The door was weathered and rough looking, which is a symbol of the strength and endurance that we have. We do not know for certain that the choices we make today will be the right ones for tomorrow. The door and key are very symbolic.

—Alyssa writes in her writers notebook about a door as a symbol.

teachers in the study, has used the writers-notebook approach in her high-school English classes to focus on daily events.

Rapid Writing

A middle-school teacher I once worked with found that those of his students who feared the blank page simply needed to be told that they had permission to write badly as a way of starting to achieve fluency. Steven Galloway, author and creative-writing teacher, agrees: "It's learning by doing and doing badly. If you don't allow yourself the possibility of writing something very, very bad, it would be hard to write something very good" (English). Rapid writing is an effective strategy that encourages fluency. For this exercise, students are given several topics and are asked to write for one to five minutes without stopping. Even if students cannot think of what to write, they are encouraged to keep the pen or pencil or fingers at the keyboard moving and at least writing, "I cannot think of anything to write about. This is hard to do but I'll keep writing until something comes to me." At the end of the time, students then count the number of words they have written and record this information on a chart in their writers notebooks.

Over time, students will chart and examine their own progress, often discovering that they are able to write more and more with each rapid-writing exercise. In addition, students can look back over their rapid writing and find topics and ideas they can write about for other purposes.

She leans forward, licks the top of her finger, and turns the page of her book. Her voice rises and falls as she reads aloud. She holds the book near her mid-section and walks back and forth across the front of the room. She touches the bridge of her nose, but her glasses have been removed and sit on top of her desk. There is little movement among the students. The light is too bright. Some students watch her, others never do.

—During a rapid-writing exercise, a student records her observations as her teacher reads aloud to the class.

DRAFTING

Drafting is the stage in The Writing Process when students actually write their texts. During the drafting stage, teachers should expect to see students writing down their ideas and perhaps stopping occasionally to read or think, or maybe even to talk to the teacher or a peer about an aspect of their writing. By this stage, students should be clear about audience and purpose, but it is possible that specific information about audience and purpose will crystallize throughout the drafting stage. Some writers, like Kit Pearson, for example, suggest focusing on telling the story during the drafting stage and thinking about audience when revising.

Separating Drafting and Correcting

Critics of current writing instruction in schools feel that, when students are taught that the most important element in writing is mechanics, students tend not to write "authentically"—that is, they are not writing "from the heart."

In order for authentic writing to occur during the drafting stage, students need to be aware that the focus of drafting should be to write down one's ideas without checking for correct spelling or thinking about mechanics. We need to make students aware of the drafting processes described by writing theorist Frank Smith, who suggests that there are two processes that occur when one writes. The first occurs when the writer attempts to commit his or her ideas to paper or computer; this he calls the *content* of the piece. The second occurs when the writer makes certain that what is being written is correct in terms of spelling, punctuation, paragraphing, and facts; this he calls *transcription*. According to Smith, these two processes oppose and interfere with each other and should be undertaken separately.

Smith observes, "The way to circumvent the pressures of transcription is to ignore them until they can be given full attention—that is, in the course of editing, when the prior demands of composition have been met" (120). He encourages all writers and teachers to use only the first process when drafting. To do this, teachers might give advice such as:

- Do not worry about spelling and punctuation during the drafting stage.
- Focus on just getting your ideas down on paper.
- Write on every other line or double space to help with revising later.
- Read your writing aloud every so often.

Rituals and Routines

Many writers feel that a specific routine is important to their writing, and perhaps even some rituals might be helpful. Teachers may find it helpful to share with their students some of the routines and rituals used by favourite authors. For instance, Natalie Goldberg takes herself for a long slow walk around the room, thinking about what she wants to say before sitting down to write. Many writers do their writing at a specific time each day and for a certain period of time. Teachers could quite easily set up such a ritual in their classrooms. Some writers like to set a mood for writing by playing a particular kind of music, reading inspirational quotes, getting a cup of tea or a glass of water, or organizing their workspace, for example. It is helpful to discuss the idea of rituals and routines with students as well as what constitutes a comfortable writing environment.

Philip Pullman, author of the well-known trilogy *His Dark Materials*, describes his typical writing routine as follows:

> I'll get up at about half past seven and take my wife a cup of tea, and have my breakfast at the kitchen table reading the paper. I'll sit down at my desk at about half past nine and work until it's time for lunch, with a break for coffee half way through. If I'm lucky I'll have written three pages by then, and I can fool about with my power tools in the afternoon. If not, it's back to the desk until the three pages are covered.
>
> I write with a ballpoint pen on A4-sized narrow-lined paper. The paper has got to have a grey or blue margin and two holes. I only write on one side, and when I've got to the bottom of the last page, I finish the sentence (or write one more) at the top of the next, so that the paper I look at each morning isn't blank. It's already beaten. That number or pages amounts, in my writing, to about 1100 words.
>
> When I've finished a story, I'll type it all on the computer, editing as I go. Then I read it all again and think it's horrible, and get very depressed. That's one of the things you have to put up with. Eventually, after a lot of fiddling, it's sort of all right, but the best I can do; and that's when I send it off to the publisher. (www.randomhouse.com/features/pullman)

Writing Exercises

Teachers need to offer a variety of writing exercises to students on a regular basis to encourage them to write. Most exercises need to be written within a certain period of time, and teachers may assign them as homework or provide class time for them. The point of having students do exercises is to help them develop the habit of drafting without concern for mechanics. There are many writing exercises available, and Linda Holeman presented a number of effective ones in the workshop she gave as part of our study (see chapter 3). I often refer to Natalie Goldberg's book *Writing Down the Bones* for my language and literacy classes with student teachers. Her book offers 15 excellent exercises (20–22), which I use with my university students:

1. Tell about the quality of light coming in through your window. Jump in and write. Don't worry if it is night and your curtains are closed or you would rather write about the light up north— just write. Go for ten minutes, fifteen, a half hour.
2. Begin with "I remember." Write lots of small memories. If you fall into one large memory, write that. Just keep going. Don't be concerned if the memory happened five seconds ago or five years ago. Everything that isn't this moment is memory coming alive again as you write. If you get stuck, just repeat the phrase "I remember" again and keep going.

3. Take something you feel strong about, whether it is positive or negative, and write about it as though you love it. Go as far as you can, writing as though you love it, then flip over and write about the same thing as though you hate it. Then write about it perfectly neutral.

4. Choose a colour—for instance, pink—and take a fifteen-minute walk. On the walk, notice wherever there is pink. Come back to your notebook and write for 15 minutes.

5. Write in different places—for example, in a laundromat, and pick up on the rhythm of the washing machines. Write at bus stops, in cafes. Write what is going on around you.

6. Give me your morning. Waking up, breakfast, walking to the bus stop. Be as specific as possible. Slow down in your mind and go over the details of the morning.

7. Visualize a place that you really love, be there, see the details. Now write about it. It could be a corner of your bedroom, an old tree you sat under one whole summer, a table at McDonald's in your neighbourhood, a place by a river. What colours are there, sounds, smells? When someone else reads it, she should know what it is like to be there. She should feel how you love it, not by your saying you love it, but by your handling of the details.

8. Write about "leaving." Approach it any way you want. Write about your divorce, leaving the house this morning, or a friend dying.

9. What is your first memory?

10. Who are the people you have loved?

11. Write about the streets of your city.

12. Describe a grandparent.

13. Write about: swimming; the stars; the most frightened you've ever been; green places; how you learned about sex; your first sexual experience; the closest you ever felt to God or nature; reading and books that have changed your life; physical endurance; a teacher you had. Don't be abstract. Write the real stuff. Be honest and detailed.

14. Take a poetry book. Open to any page, grab a line, write it down, and continue from there. A friend calls it "writing off the page." If you begin with a great line, it helps because you start right off from a lofty place. "I will die in Paris, on a rainy day.... It will be a Thursday," by the poet Cesar Vallejo. "I will die on Monday at eleven o'clock, on Friday at three o'clock in South Dakota riding a tractor, in Brooklyn in a delicatessen," on and on. Every time you get stuck, just rewrite your first line and keep going. Re-writing the first line gives you a whole new start and a chance for another direction—"I don't want to die and I don't care if I'm in Paris or Moscow or Youngstown, Ohio."

15. What kind of animal are you? Do you think you are really a cow, chipmunk, fox, or a horse underneath?

The point of such exercises is not only to give students the opportunity to write on a regular basis but also to find topics they might not otherwise have been interested in. In one grade-11 class I observed, a student told me that, when she was doing the writing exercises assigned to her by the student teacher I was observing, she found that she enjoyed writing about future possibilities in her life. She said that the activity helped her think about what she might study in university and set goals for that. This was a positive outcome of a writing exercise and not necessarily one anticipated by the student or the student teacher.

Modelling

When you, as teacher, have your students watch as you draft a piece of writing, you help take away some of the mystery that many of them may associate with writing. You can use the white board, a smart board, an overhead projector, or a computer with a large screen to model the process. (If you use a smart board, it is important to ensure that all students can see it; smart boards often give off a sheen, making details difficult to see.) You might incorporate a think-aloud strategy while drafting, sharing your thoughts about the writing as they occur. Modelling is an important strategy in writing instruction, even for teachers who are not confident about their own writing abilities. Modelling helps teachers empathize with the demands of writing faced by teens in school.

I often employ the modelling strategy when I am asked to conduct a writers workshop for students. I draft using a computer (my work projected onto a large screen). I often start out by writing about getting to the school on that particular day. For example:

> This morning when I woke up, I knew I would be coming here to your school to work with you on writing. So, I began thinking of topics I might write about. As I was sitting at the kitchen table, having my second cup of coffee, I noticed the calendar on the fridge that lists all the family activities for the month. There, on the calendar for the month of June, was a picture of the Rocky Mountains. They looked beautiful—rugged, strong, and snowy. I thought that I might write about the mountains and some of the times I've spend there with my family skiing. One of our ski holidays involved teaching our younger daughter, Erin, how to ski using a tow rope and a smallish hill at the ski resort. It was hard work.

Then I tell the students that I need a first line to begin this piece of writing and ask for suggestions. This demonstrates the value of talking and getting input from others during the drafting stage. Eventually, we settle on the following: "I looked out the cabin window at the fluffy white snow, anticipating a day of fun and excitement atop Big Mountain."

Students appreciate demonstrations of the drafting process; they are able to see immediately when the writing works and when it does not. They also learn that drafting is fraught with stops and starts.

Reading Aloud

Reading aloud from exemplary texts is an excellent strategy that teachers can use to show students how tone and vocabulary can be used effectively. It can give them a chance to think of ways they might emulate an established writer's style. Teachers should occasionally encourage students to respond to the reading by emulating that style.

When students start to read their own writing aloud, either to themselves or to an audience, they begin to develop self-assessment. They learn to examine their own writing and evaluate its effectiveness in meeting their goals, which in turn leads to a feeling of control over their own writing.

Examining What Writers Say

One teacher I know often uses an extract from Barbara Kingsolver's book of essays called *Small Wonder* to demonstrate how established writers work and what they think about writing in general:

> For me to love a work of fiction, it must survive my harpy eye on all accounts: It will tell me something remarkable, it will be beautifully executed, and it will be nested in truth. The latter I mean literally; I can't abide fiction that fails to get its facts straight. I've tossed aside stories because of botched Spanish or French phrases uttered by putative native speakers who were not supposed to be toddlers or illiterates. (212)

This teacher asks students to write down what they think Kingsolver means in this short excerpt and how they might apply her advice to their own writing. The point of this writing activity is to help students think the way writers do when they are drafting their own pieces. In her book entitled *Bird by Bird,* Anne Lamott makes it clear that writing is both exhilarating and fraught with difficulties: "[I tell my students that] they will have days at the desk of frantic boredom, of angry hopelessness, of wanting to quit forever, and there will be days when it feels like they have caught and are riding a wave" (xxix).

Practising Leads

The opening sentences of a piece of writing very quickly show the reader whether it is worth reading or not. During the drafting stage, it is helpful to encourage students to examine a variety of leads from books they read and decide for themselves which ones pull them into the text and which ones do not. One teacher-librarian I know loved to teach about leads by reading from *Looking for X* by Deborah Ellis. Before beginning to read the book, she would warn her students that the book started off with a "zinger." Then she opened the book to the first page and read "My mom used to be a stripper" and immediately closed it. Students cried out immediately for more. The same thing occurs in classrooms when teachers read the opening line of Charles Dickens's *A Tale of Two Cities,* which begins, "It was the best of times. It was the worst of times." Using this approach helps students recognize the importance of leads in their own writing as a way of hooking readers and getting them to continue reading.

To teach the importance of leads, teachers can provide examples for students to examine. For instance, if students are writing essays, they can be encouraged to see how different leads can cause different reader responses. The teacher might ask the students to consider how a question at the beginning of a piece might get a reader interested—for example, "What would you do if you found out that your best friend had started smoking?" Or an exclamatory sentence—for example, "Seventy percent of all teens report that they have smoked at some time in their lives!"

When students are doing narrative writing, teachers can discuss with students the value of beginning a story with dialogue—for example:

"Where do you think we should hide it?" Matt asked me.
"I don't know yet, but someone is coming. Shhhh!" I answered.

Drafting Conferences

While it is customary to think of drafting as a quiet endeavour, a time when students are busy working independently on their own writing, we need to make sure that the drafting stage also includes time for students to talk to one another or the teacher.

The point of the conference is to help the student continue writing, so remaining too long with one student can be counterproductive—the student can become too reliant on the teacher. Sometimes a student believes that he or she must know precisely what will be written before getting started. We need to let them know that this may not be the case, that a draft is not a final product. Many writers decide what will occur in a piece only while they are writing. It is necessary to tell students that it is fine to make mistakes in a draft, fine to change their minds, fine to find the focus while writing. We need to encourage students not to delete or throw away their drafts.

Conferences can occur between teacher and student (or students), or they can occur among students. Colin (see chapter 2), commented that he appreciated the opportunity to work with other students in his classroom to get ideas for writing and to work through periods of difficulty in his writing.

Nancie Atwell has designed several sets of conference questions that work well to help the writer begin drafting, one of which looks like this:

- What is your writing about?
- What is your purpose in writing this piece?
- Tell me what you are trying to say.
- Who are you writing this for?
- What are you interested in? Can you tell me more about that?
- I think your main idea is: _____. Is that correct?

Writing to One Specific Person

The strategy of writing to an audience of just one person can be very effective for students who are unsure about how to move from prewriting to drafting. (In the same way, novice public speakers are often advised to speak primarily to one member of the audience.) That person could be a friend or family member, a book or television-show character, or a teacher. It should be someone the student feels comfortable with. One journalist I read about, when he realized that he was not going to be able to make his deadline, decided to send his notes to his managing editor so that someone else could write the article. As he prepared his notes (with one person as the focus), he suddenly found that he was able to write the article and meet his deadline. One grade-9 student who tried this strategy wrote the following:

Dear Mom,

I am trying to write a story about our recent visit to Vancouver Island last summer. I am not too sure where to start, but some of the things I want to write about are the antique shops, the kayaks we rented, visiting Aunt Mary, and the ferry ride over. Remember how rough it was when we went over on the ferry? Maybe that's where I'll begin the story, since that's how the trip began. We waited in line for over an hour...

This student continued drafting and produced more than three handwritten pages about his summer trip.

REVISING

Revising is defined as that stage in The Writing Process "of adding, deleting, substituting, or rearranging material to improve a text" (Saddler 20). The writer must reread the text and ask questions about its clarity, form, function, purpose, and audience. Such questions are difficult, because the writer must follow up and work further with the text. While many skilled writers engage in revision on an ongoing basis, that is, not just when they have a completed first draft, many struggling writers lack the skills or the motivation to do it. They often make only surface changes, such as adding punctuation, to demonstrate (even to themselves) that they have revised their writing.

Revising is the stage of The Writing Process that teachers say is the most difficult in which to engage students. English teacher Shelly Smede sums up the frustration felt by many teachers:

I was frustrated for many years. I spent days helping eighth graders prewrite, then hurried them through the drafting and revision phase, often sending them home to do most of that.... Students would turn in piles of poor, disorganized, and uninspired papers, and I would spend hours making comments and suggestions to my student writers....I always requested that students check my suggestions and resubmit their work.... The few students who accepted this offer ignored my ideas.... Revision, it seemed, must be beyond the reach of average thirteen-year-olds and at the very most was a chore they refused to do on their own. (118)

Teachers often lament that students would rather begin new pieces of writing than to revisit previous writing. But many authors say that revising is the most important stage of their writing process. Some say that it represents as much as 90 percent of their writing time.

In order to help students engage in revising their own writing, it is necessary to help them see the value of revising. As Saddler points out, "before teaching students how to revise, you may have to teach them why they need to revise" (22). In many cases, revising is viewed by students as simply more work; they have already worked very hard to produce the piece in the first place. Teachers and researchers have developed several strategies that can be used in the classroom to help students understand the value of revising: rereading, using revision checklists, engaging in conferences, colour-coding, writing reflective letters. These strategies are best done during class time, when the teacher is available to help students work through difficulties and questions as they arise.

Rereading

One of the simplest methods of encouraging students to revise is to have them reread their writing. Teachers can help students understand the value of rereading one's work by taking the time in class to read aloud from a variety of texts. They need to read slowly and deliberately, focusing on the sound of the language—its vocabulary and rhythm. Students will begin to appreciate the beauty of language and take pride in their own words.

Students can reread their writing to themselves, to another person, or into a tape recorder to hear how it sounds. They often detect inconsistencies, missing information, and incorrect vocabulary just by listening to themselves read their work. One of the students in our study said that she finds it easier to reread her work when it is on a computer screen and that she does not reread her handwritten material as often.

Using Revision Checklists

There is a variety of checklists and guides that students can use to revise their writing. It is important to note that, while checklists can be very helpful, most are generic, and so teachers need to be aware that checklists often need to be modified. There is one checklist, however (and this one does not need modification), that is particularly helpful for students who have never revised before. It is called Three-Column Revision (Smede). Students make three columns on a piece of paper. They label the first column Sentence Beginnings and record the first word of each sentence. Students are often surprised to find that they begin their sentences in similar ways and are encouraged to add some variety to the beginnings of their sentences. They label the second column Sentence Lengths and record the number of words in each sentence. Again, students are often surprised to find out that most of their sentences have between nine and twelve words in them and are encouraged to vary the lengths of their sentences. This change to the rhythm of the piece makes it that much more interesting to read. Most students are excited to see how good their writing sounds once they change the rhythm. They label the third column Verbs and record the verbs they use. Smede notes that the Three-Column Revision checklist helps students learn to replace repetitive action words with "vivid, more descriptive verbs" (118). Similar types of activities can be used for helping students check their own writing for other aspects of usage such as verb tenses. (See appendix C and figure 4.5.) Most important, revision checklists are effective only if they are used authentically. Teachers should have students use their own writing for revision exercises. In doing so, they help students feel that they are working on the "real" job of writing, not just learning an abstract principle.

Sentence Beginnings	Sentence Lengths	Verbs
The	6	is
In	7	having
The	6	can
Then	8	is

Figure 4.5. A sample of a student's use of the Three-Column Revision checklist

Engaging in Revision Conferences

A revision conference can provide an opportunity for students to reread their text aloud for an audience. An audience—made up of peers, teachers, or parents—may be able to detect problems with a text that the writer does not see or hear. For this reason, conferences with peers, teachers, and parents can be helpful to the revision process. Anne Lamott says:

> One of the best writers I know has a wife who reads everything he writes and tells him when she loves it and when she doesn't, why it does or doesn't work for her. She is almost like an equal partner in the process. (165)

Helpful peer conferencing requires that the "critic" receive some instruction. To do this, the teacher can model a conference with one or two students to show how they should conduct themselves. For example, the teacher could sit with two students and ask one of them to read his or her writing to the other. The second student would act as critic (VanDeWeghe). The critic would have a copy of the text and could underline or highlight aspects of the text that are confusing or require further explanation. The student writer would provide explanations during the conference and then make notes about where to change the text. The two students would then switch roles and repeat the process. Both students would then work on their own to make the changes. Later, they would participate in another conference to show how the changes had been incorporated and explain how they affected the text.

At the end of the process, to keep track of the kinds of revision each student is working on, the teacher asks the critic for a written summary of the conference discussion. (See appendices D and E for summary guidelines, adapted from Saddler.)

The writer reads the conference summary sheet before making revisions. It is important that the writer remain in control of the process and decide whether or not to follow the critic's suggestions.

Using Colour-Codes and Index Cards

One aspect of student writing that frequently requires revision is its organization. This is particularly true for non-fiction. One strategy that can help solve problems of organization is colour-coding.

Students need to have a copy of their draft at hand and several differently coloured highlighters. The student highlights the first sentence in each paragraph with one colour. The topic sentence in the first paragraph might be blue, for example, and the colour for the topic sentence in the second paragraph might be yellow. The students then examine each topic sentence to see if it adequately expresses the overall idea of the paragraph. Next, the student reads the draft and finds any sentences that relate to that topic sentence and highlights them in the same colour as the topic sentence. Students can now readily view sentences that may be placed in the wrong paragraph and can move them in the next draft.

The same idea can be used with index cards. Students rewrite the topic sentence of each paragraph on index cards, which are labelled and numbered (Paragraph 1, Paragraph 2, and so on). The student rereads the text and writes all the sentences that go with each topic sentence onto the pertinent index card. Sentences that are difficult to place are more easily moved around when using this strategy. This strategy can be time-consuming when students are using a hard copy of the writing, but its "hands-on" nature can make it valuable for students who need concrete guidance in organizing a piece of writing. The same strategy can be used on the computer with the copy-and-paste function.

Writing a Reflective Letter

While teachers, peers, and parents can assist the student writer in making revisions, ultimately it is the writer who needs to see the value of revision and be motivated to do so. In order to find out how students are thinking about revision and their roles as revisers, it is helpful for teachers to include some form of reflection in their writing instruction.

Dawn Swartzendruber-Putnam, a high-school English teacher, uses a reflective-writing exercise as a way to ensure that writers think critically about their writing. She has her students use the letter form to comment upon their pieces of writing on a regular basis, but particularly at the end of a unit. Her directions for the exercise encourage students to tell the teacher about the process of writing the piece and to make visible any aspects that may not be evident to her. She says:

> This is your chance to tell me anything I should know before I give you my comments. Nothing feels worse than being criticized for something you already know isn't working well, or to not be commended for something you really thought was great. Let me know what you think and I can help you. (90)

In order to ensure that the letters she receives are thoughtful and detailed, Swartzendruber-Putnam models several aspects of the letter-writing process. She provides examples of students' letters that do more than comment superficially on the writing. When a student says that he likes the way he organized the piece, for example, she would say that the comment needs amplification; she wants to know why he thinks the organization is good. An appropriate reflection would include a list of aspects that he thinks are good. He might say, for example, that he used a format that included an introduction, several developmental paragraphs, and a conclusion, and that the conclusion included references to each of the major points in the body. This type of reflection shows that the student understood the vocabulary of writing and that he recognized how a good piece of writing differed from a not-so-good piece. One student writes,

> My growth has been quite significant because I have learned to have confidence in my writing and I have learned I can write a variety of pieces that are very different yet still interesting. My piece on the movie *Swing Kids* was informative because I researched WWII and used that information in my writing. Without that additional information, my writing would not have been as strong.

This reflective letter shows the student's understanding of what he does as a writer beyond having created the actual product. It also shows his ability to use writing terminology correctly.

Take the time to effectively model the writing of a reflective letter.

EDITING

Editing is the stage of The Writing Process when mechanical errors in the writing are fixed. The editor attends to spelling, punctuation, capitalization, and grammar. It is not easy, as 19-year-old author Christopher Paolini indicates about the editing of his best-selling book, *Eragon*:

> The real torture with *Eragon* came in the editing. I discovered that editing is really another word for someone ruthlessly tearing apart your work with a big smile, all the while telling you that it will make the book so much better. And it did, though it felt like splinters of hot bamboo being driven into my tender eyeballs. ("Author Spotlight")

It is important that, as teachers, we not forget that teenage writers (indeed, all writers) are intensely sensitive about their own work.

At the editing stage, it often happens that the content and organization of the piece of writing are, for the most part, set, and the work requires few if any changes. When the writer spends a great deal of time on revision, it is likely that many of the mechanical errors will already have been corrected. Nonetheless, it is helpful to make sure that the editing stage does occur, so that students can understand the mechanics of language and the effect that correct language has on communication. Writers often discuss among themselves the importance of good editing skills; many credit their English teachers with having given them a strong sense of the correctness of language. (It is especially important that students learn to spell. While being a good speller is not necessarily a sign of high intelligence, readers tend to assume that texts that contain spelling errors have been written by people with a poor education or who are careless.)

Many teachers warn that it is important to keep editing in perspective. When teachers allow editing to become the focus of learning to write, students can forget that the purpose of writing is to say something to a reader. Good writing is much more than just using correct spelling, punctuation, and grammar. Indeed, some writers deliberately break the rules. Frank McCourt is a superb writer, and his book *Angela's Ashes* shows how very experienced writers can employ grammatical errors to create believable characters and dialogue. McCourt writes his novel in the first person, from a young boy's perspective while living in dire poverty with his family in Ireland. When students are exposed to a variety of texts, some that follow and some that break editing rules, they learn how to write their own meaningful pieces. But, more important, when they know the rules, they can articulate the reasons for sometimes breaking them.

There are a number of effective strategies that help writers improve their editing skills. I treat three of them here: the editors station, the mini-lesson, and the editing checklist.

The Editors Station

Setting up an editors station in the classroom is one way of stressing the importance of the editing stage. An effective editors station is set up in a quiet place in the classroom or in the library or computer room and accommodates two to five students at a time. It contains a variety of print and electronic resources that students can use to edit their own or another's piece of writing. Print resources include dictionaries, thesauri, spelling workbooks, and writing handbooks; electronic resources include the spell-check, grammar-check, and thesaurus functions on a computer. There is also a variety of print resources that focus on editing.

Teachers can introduce students to a set of editing symbols that are designed to simplify the editing process and help make editorial instructions clear (see figure 4.6). They can challenge eager students by introducing them to proofreading symbols as well (a more complex and detailed part of the editing stage). Reluctant writers may get to know only a few symbols. The editors station is a valuable strategy, however, only if students have been taught how to use editing symbols.

There is some evidence that shows that, if a student leaves a piece of writing for a time (a few days to two weeks), he or she is more likely to see what needs to be edited and may be more motivated to do so. Therefore, it may be necessary to give students time after completing a draft before they visit the editors station.

(An effective way of proofreading a piece of writing for spelling, by the way, is to start at the end and move backward; the editor can focus his or her attention on the word and not the meaning.)

The Mini-Lesson

One of the best ways to teach students how, when, and why to edit is to present mini-lessons, in which teachers can present specific aspects of editing in a direct, short, and focused manner. It is useful to use student writing for mini-lessons (either current students or previous students who have donated their work for teaching purposes). Sometimes it is appropriate to use the teacher's own writing. The teacher can choose to

EDITING SYMBOLS	
Symbol	Meaning
∧	Insert a letter or word.
/	Insert a space.
⌒	Reverse letters or words.
☉	Insert a comma.
⌒	Delete
¶	Make a new paragraph.

Figure 4.6. Editing symbols

teach a mini-lesson to the entire class or, perhaps, to a small group of students who might be struggling with a particular writing skill.

An effective mini-lesson should take between 10 and 15 minutes, although more time may be spent if necessary. The teacher begins by indicating the skill that will be discussed and why. The teacher presents examples in which the skill is used correctly and examples where it is used incorrectly. For instance, if students are working on subject-verb agreement, it is useful to show how confusing a piece of writing can be when subject and verb do not agree (see figure 4.7).

The teacher can occasionally provide extra practice of a particular skill, using a worksheet or the white board. However, because skill development does not often transfer to one's own writing, it is not a good idea to spend a great deal of time on the mechanics of writing in the absence of real writing samples. It is always a good idea to capture teachable moments when working on a student's writing.

The Editing Checklist

There are many editing checklists that teachers and students can use. These can be used for self-editing or for peer- or teacher-editing. Generally, it is useful for the student to learn how to edit for him- or herself, a much better scenario than having the teacher make all the corrections. (See appendices F and G.)

PUBLISHING

Publishing is the stage in The Writing Process when writers produce a final piece to share with an audience. However, not everything that a student writes needs to be published. Indeed, the pressure to publish may destroy any interest in writing. Instead, students should examine the writing they

---

Subject-Verb Agreement

Incorrect usage: The drama teacher said that *the students* have a role as *an active participant* in the school play.

Correct usage: The drama teacher said that *the students* have a role as *active participants* in the school play.

Figure 4.7. A mini-lesson chart showing the incorrect and correct versions of a sentence

have done at the end of a unit or a month and choose one or two pieces that they would like to publish or have marked by the teacher. They can write on a regular basis, they can "write badly" sometimes, and they can pick and choose what they think is the best. And they should keep on writing. Anne Lamott observes:

> I just try to warn people who hope to get published that publication is not all that it is cracked up to be. But writing is. Writing has so much to give, so much to teach, so many surprises. That thing you had to force yourself to do—the actual part of writing— turns out to be the best part.... The act of writing turns out to be its own reward. (xxvi)

Students should keep all their writing in a portfolio, either as hard copies or on a computer (and make sure that they make backup copies that are stored on an external disk). Students should think of their writing portfolios as a place for all their writing (an active portfolio), but they should also be encouraged to create a showcase portfolio at the end of a course or school year (a passive portfolio). Students' passive portfolios can be displayed at school events such as career fairs, parent evenings, and fine-arts presentations. (See chapter 5 for more about writing portfolios.)

Ways to Publish Student Writing

There is a variety of ways for writing to be published. For teens, the publication of their writing need not be "showy." Indeed, a showy publication might dampen the interest of many in writing rather than encourage it. However, it is important to ensure that students' writing is acknowledged somehow. Some popular ways include:
- reading one's writing aloud to another person or a small group of people
- typing the writing on the computer
- displaying the writing in the classroom or some other public place
- placing the writing on a school or class website
- developing one's own weblog to post published writing
- entering writing contests
- publishing writing on websites designed for teen writing
- creating a class anthology of students' work
- publishing a class or school newspaper with student writing
- creating posters that visually represent one's writing

- sharing writing with parents at a school open house
- displaying student writing at teacher events such as conferences and work days
- printing final copies on interesting paper

Make sure that students are comfortable with displaying and sharing their writing with others before you ask them to do so. Teens, like many of the rest of us, can be deeply affected by the reactions of others, so we must ensure that a positive climate exists in which students can share their writing.

Real Audiences

One of the most disheartening findings in research on teaching writing is that most of the writing a student produces is done only for the teacher; for many teens, there is no sense of a real audience. The students in our study indicated that their interest in writing developed because they could see the effect that something they wrote had on an audience. It made the reader laugh, gasp, or want to know more. This tells us that we need to be more diligent in providing real audiences for our student writers.

Assessing and Evaluating Student Writing

"The worst part of writing," Virginia Woolf observed in her diary, quoting a friend, "is that one depends so much upon praise." Which is to say that a writer, like any other artist, is continually offering his or her work for public assessment, and it is only human to want to be praised for one's efforts rather than blamed. (Lodge 102)

Goal of this Chapter

My goal in this chapter is to identify the difference between assessing writing for learning and evaluating writing to judge it. Given the sheer volume of marking that secondary school teachers have to do, this is especially important. I discuss several ways to accomplish both assessment and evaluation by focusing on holistic procedures, conferences, portfolios, rubrics, and standardized tests.

Writer Natalie Goldberg explains that her approach to writing in school was as a "goody-two-shoes": "I wanted my teachers to like me. I learned commas, colons, semicolons. I wrote compositions with clear sentences that were dull and boring" (*Writing* 1). Goldberg believes that students often learn aspects of writing in school that their teachers do not intend and that it is through effective and well-considered assessment and evaluation practices that students learn that writing is also about expression and effective communication. Key to effective assessment and evaluation of writing is providing the writer with enough praise to feel acknowledged and enough constructive feedback to feel encouraged. According to author and teacher Erika Lindemann, the teacher's two most important jobs when looking at students' writing are: (1) making an initial diagnosis of students' strengths and weaknesses; and (2) guiding and focusing feedback to students as they write. This is referred to as "assessment for learning"; it focuses on enhancing learning and on student involvement in his or her own learning (Black et al.). The teacher tells the student what he or she has done well and then identifies what can be improved. After an assessment, teachers need to provide opportunities for students to reflect, rewrite their drafts, and implement suggested changes.

Evaluation, on the other hand, is a judgment about the writing and results in a grade. There is less opportunity for students to change their writing and implement suggested changes. My own experience of grading student writing at the university level is that students see the grade as the last step of their writing and seldom read or reflect on any comments on the piece. Writing experts agree that, while grades are a necessary part of education, teachers need to place greater emphasis on assessment for learning when teaching writing to teens.

Some experts talk about the destructive nature of evaluating student writing. Peter Elbow, for instance, warns, "Students often get so dependent upon grades that they feel grades are the only reason to write—sometimes even refusing if there is no grade" (397). Ruth Butler's work with assessment and evaluation is instructive. In one of her studies, she set up three different kinds of feedback: marks, comments, and a combination of both marks and comments. Results showed that most gains in learning occurred with the group that received comments only. Surprising? Not really, when you consider that students do not often read comments when a mark has been given. Butler's results suggest that the best way to ensure that students do read comments in the assessment process is to forego the mark.

I believe that it is important to provide frequent assessment, through written comments, conferences, self-assessment, and peer assessments, and to give students more opportunities to practise writing. It is not necessary to mark every piece of writing that your students produce, but it is helpful to provide a variety of audiences, such as bringing in others to listen and react to the students' writing.

The assessment and evaluation strategies I present here can help ease the overwhelming volume of writing that teachers have to deal with every week. I call them holistic procedures; they allow the teacher to make fairly quick and informed decisions about how well a piece of writing meets a set of criteria. Conferences are another helpful way for teachers to gain insight into the student writers' perspectives as they proceed. Portfolios are helpful too. They hold a student's collection of writing over time in one place and allow both students and teachers to view growth and set goals for improvement. Rubrics are another way. They are scoring guides (various quality indicators) created by the teacher, and sometimes the students, to set the level of performance. Standardized tests are another; they evaluate student performance in a manner that allows teachers, school districts, and governments to check on students' levels of achievement in writing.

HOLISTIC PROCEDURES

Holistic assessment allows the teacher to examine a piece of writing in a time-efficient manner and make judgments about skill level in order to offer helpful advice. While there are many holistic procedures that teachers can use to assess a piece of writing, one in particular stands out, and that is the one offered by Timothy Shanahan, citing the early work of James Howard. The point of this procedure is to grade papers rather than to correct them.

Teachers read the papers submitted by the students and divide them into the grade designations according to set criteria, which may or may not include student involvement. For instance, teachers may choose to divide the papers into three grade groups: *A/B, C,* and *D.* Generally, an *A* or *B* designation means that the paper demonstrates a full, or almost full, understanding of the concept being studied. It also contains language that is mostly correct for the stage of the student's development. A paper with a *C* designation contains some errors, perhaps in content and/or in the writing, but is mostly correct. Finally, a *D* means that there are serious problems in content and writing. Next, the teacher examines the *C* and *D* papers to gain insight into the kinds of errors that occurred, perhaps further dividing the papers into categories. This process allows the teacher to provide instruction where it is needed without having spent a great deal of time correcting details.

Shanahan points out that it is necessary to share with the students the criteria used for this type of grading. He writes, "The grades give students a clear picture of where they stand, and the criteria give them a clear understanding of the distance between the new and the known" (72). Many experts in assessment and evaluation argue not only that the criteria should be clear before the writing begins but also that students themselves should be asked to participate in the creation of those criteria.

Holistic procedures need to be used in conjunction with other procedures, however, as they tend to give "bottom-line" (or "big-picture") feedback to the student and do not pinpoint specific areas for improvement.

CONFERENCES

While writing conferences are used throughout The Writing Process (during revising and editing), they also have a role to play when a piece of writing is finished. When their work is marked, students can have questions about the teacher's grade and feedback, and a conference is the perfect situation in which to answer them. One student confided to me that, when she received her writing back from the teacher, it had the following marks on it: C-8, SS-5, V-5, M-6, O-6 = 25/50. The student was too embarrassed to admit that, while she understood the numbers, and especially the final mark, she did not understand the shorthand used to describe the categories. Unfortunately, she did not talk to the teacher about this and was, therefore, unable to make improvements to her writing for the next assignment. This happens all too often in middle- and high-school classrooms.

A writing conference is a good way to clarify many items that either the teacher or the student needs to talk about. The conference is a less threatening environment than a one-on-one meeting. During a conference, students can ask questions and share concerns, and even clear up misunderstandings that might occur. In order to help ensure that the conference does not become a venue in which the teacher does all the talking, it is helpful to have students prepare for the conference by using a conference guide (see appendix H).

A conference guide is useful to all students but may be particularly helpful to students who would not otherwise seek out the teacher with their questions and concerns. The guide also provides a record over time of student questions and ideas for their writing that can be revisited and discussed again.

Conferences also provide opportunities for students to clarify teachers' comments. For instance, general comments such as "Good," "Well done," or "Needs Improvement" do not clearly tell the student what he or she can do to improve or what to keep doing, and these terms can be clarified in conference. Another important feature of conferencing is the teacher's commitment to listening to the student as he or she explains his understanding of the assignment and intentions while completing it. This clearly demonstrates the role of the students as active participants in the learning process and the role of the teacher to support this process (Black et al.).

PORTFOLIOS

The portfolio is the heart of the writing instruction program. It is a representation of students' development over time and of the writing program being offered by the teacher(s). The portfolio allows for both assessment for learning and for evaluation. Teachers examine the portfolio and talk to the students to determine what to teach and how to assist the writer to learn new skills. Teachers also make judgments about the quality of students' work and create lessons to meet the variety of skill levels among the students in the class.

Portfolios are valid indicators of three important aspects of learning: (1) student progress (what students are learning to do), (2) accomplishment (what they can do), and (3) reflection about next steps or goals (what they will do). Current writing instruction must accommodate the explosion of technology in schools and around the world. Teachers need to be aware of developing hardware and software in order help writers fit into a world of up-to-date technologies. (And they need to stress, early in the school year, the importance of maintaining both a hard copy and an electronic copy, just in case technology fails.)

These days, the computer is the best place to collect, record, fine-tune, and store pieces of writing on an ongoing basis. However, it is very important that all writing be backed up in print form or on disc. Organizing the various stages of one's writing is very easy on a computer. Students can place drafts in one folder, pieces for revision and editing in another, and finished pieces in yet another. They can file comments and reflections alongside the pieces they relate to or in a separate folder. There are many ways of keeping one's writing well organized on a computer. Students need to take care when naming the files to make sure that they reflect the correct version. They need to keep a log that includes the title of each piece, the date each was begun, and the date it was finished (unless the student has decided to abandon the piece). There should be a folder for (or a link to) self-, peer-, and teacher-evaluation forms that are associated with the pieces.

A legal-sized folder that contains two pockets on the inside is an excellent container for a hard-copy portfolio. Students can add visual representations to the outside of the portfolio to personalize it. There needs to be a page glued to the inside flap of the folder to record the student's writing throughout the month, unit, semester, or year. This page should include the date that each piece of writing was begun, the date it was completed (unless it has been abandoned), and the title. Drafts and mind maps, K-W-L charts, and other documentation can be kept in one pocket. Published pieces can go into the other pocket until they are handed in to the teacher or shared with an audience. Self-evaluations, as well as peer-assessment and teacher assessments, should be attached to the finished pieces.

The teacher needs to spend at least one class period each month with students going over the content and the process of maintaining the portfolio. During this class, students talk about what they have written, what areas of their writing are working, and what areas need improvement. They review their own work and that of their peers. They discuss the challenges of revising and editing and share ideas for prewriting and drafting. By visiting the portfolio each month with these goals in mind, students develop the ability to monitor and manage their own learning. This kind of interaction with the content of the portfolio is invaluable in helping students develop a sense of ownership about their writing.

Storing one's writing electronically has several advantages over storing it as hard copy. First, there is space: there is no end to the amount of writing that can be stored and easily accessed at any given time on a computer. Second, there is longevity: writing can be saved, not just over the course of a semester, but over several years. This allows students the opportunity to see the "big picture" and reflect on their development as writers over a long period of time. Teachers who are fortunate enough to work with the same students in several different courses throughout middle school or high school can take note of their students' development over time, an often gratifying experience. Third, there is ease of storage: students can store assessments (self, peer, and teacher) to use when a piece of writing is completed. It was very helpful to me, as a researcher, when the teens in my study could easily locate and print out writing that they had produced two and three years earlier. This likely would not have been possible had they produced only hard copies of their writing.

We encourage students to write both at school and at home. But, unless the movement of students' writing between home and school in electronic format can be achieved easily for most students, it might be desirable for them to keep their portfolios in hard-copy format. I recommend that students use memory sticks to store their portfolios when moving back and forth between home computers and school computers. However, we need to teach students to take precautions to ensure that we do not spread viruses while doing so.

Active and Passive Portfolios

An active portfolio is one that is kept by students as a working document. Its contents "illustrate a developmental story of a student's writing over time" (Wilcox 35). Many writers believe in the importance of never throwing away anything that they write. We need to encourage students to keep their writing over time, so that they may reflect on their own growth as writers. They might also reread it, revise it, and find a place for it in another piece, later on.

A passive portfolio is one used to showcase students' final products. Its usefulness in showing development is limited. However, a showcase portfolio can be very positive for a student. The audience for a showcase portfolio could be parents, teachers, or administrators. Portfolios can be shown in a school's display case in the same way that athletic awards are. Showcase portfolios can also be used when students enter writing competitions or apply for awards and scholarships. Some universities ask that students present writing portfolios for admission into creative-writing programs.

Portfolio Letters

Teachers are beginning to see the value of incorporating a form of self-assessment into their own assessment and evaluation procedures. Students need to have opportunities for metacognitive reflection (the ability to think about one's thinking) if they are to participate fully in their own development as writers. The portfolio letter is one way to encourage metacognition.

The portfolio letter is similar to the reflective letter (see chapter 4). The main difference is in timing—that is, the point during The Writing Process when the letter is called for. While the reflective letter is written during the process and refers primarily to a single piece of writing, the portfolio letter is written at the end of the process and refers to a number of pieces collected over time (Swartzendruber-Putnam).

Teachers need to present examples of what an effective portfolio letter contains: a student's own evaluation of his or her writing collection, some references to how The Writing Process has been used, and a demonstration of the student's own knowledge and abilities. Unlike the reflective letter, which is meant to inspire future writing, the portfolio letter is graded by the teacher.

Students may also find it helpful to confer individually with the teacher to improve their own reflective processes. Teachers and students share the responsibility for learning in such situations. When students learn to write reflective letters, they are also learning to take on more responsibility for their own learning and are likely to view their writing as valuable and worthwhile.

Holly's portfolio letter says, in part:

> I notice that in my character description I write about "Haley" as if I am describing someone I do not actually know well. I only give a physical description of her, which does not let the reader know her very well or who she is. I am disappointed when I read

this assignment now, because I liked it when I wrote it. Now I see that it is a very superficial description and it does not make the reader want to know who she is. If I was going to describe a character now I would include little things like how she wears her hair to partly cover her face to hide her insecurity about really facing people. I would not go into such detail about the colour and fabric of her blouse, which did nothing to tell the reader more about Haley as a person. This description did not move the story along at all.

Later in her portfolio letter, Holly refers to the source of her new-found knowledge about character:

I am really enjoying reading books by Laurie Halse Anderson, because she tells the reader things about her characters that you can't really just see. I mean you just know that Melinda is not taking care of her appearance throughout the book because of how other people treat her.

Holly is able to discuss her writing thoughtfully, and she understands what she is learning as a writer. Moreover, she is able to reflect upon the source of her learning.

RUBRICS AND TEACHER COMMENTS

When discussing the concepts of *assessment for learning* and *evaluation*, it is impossible not to also mention *rubrics*. Among evaluation scholars, rubrics have been touted as the most important strategy for ensuring unambiguous marking in areas typically plagued with ambiguity, like writing.

A rubric is a scoring guide that specifies the level of performance expected from a student. The guide describes various levels of quality and/or includes a set of criteria, as well as a numerical or grade equivalent. Top-level quality could be assigned a grade of *A* or, perhaps, a score of 5/5. The criteria might be, for example: This piece of writing shows a complete understanding of the topic. It is organized according to major themes in paragraphs. It includes an effective introduction and ending that engage the reader.

Teachers and students alike appear to appreciate the high level of specificity that rubrics can provide. Teacher Adele Fiderer says, "If you're like me, you've probably grappled with the task of assigning the right score for a student's essay, presentation, or project. Rubrics have helped me score complex work products such as these quickly and fairly" (*Rubrics*). The rubric clearly states what counts and even outlines gradations of quality. (See appendix I.)

Used wisely, rubrics are very helpful in reducing the amount of time teachers spend on marking. However, they are often time-consuming and sometimes tricky to create. Teachers must use crystal-clear language to describe the various levels of quality. For instance, if the teacher describes an *A*-quality paper by noting that the beginning is "creative," then the term *creative* must be defined. And we must remember that many of the qualities of fine writing cannot be defined. Overuse of rubrics leads to the expectation that writing is simply putting the correct words in the correct order, and this is not true. David Narter, a high-school English teacher, cautions teachers about over-using rubrics to assess and evaluate a student's writing. He notes:

> The rubric's obvious shortcoming in the English classroom is its inability to measure the idiosyncrasies any quality writing teacher recognizes and encourages in his or her students. (67)

It is important to note that, regardless of how specific a rubric might be, it is impossible to completely eliminate subjectivity in arriving at a mark or level designation for a student's piece of writing. A rubric will make assessment and evaluation *appear* objective, but the teacher's choice of level is still subjective.

Writing that is meaningful and affects its audience is not always technically correct writing; writing, in a creative sense, often cannot be spelled out in a rubric. But rubrics can provide guidelines to assist students as they begin the writing assignment.

One of the participants in my study offers this advice to writing teachers:

> In middle school and grade 12, we had grades and comments. I found that comments helped tremendously and told me how to improve for next time. In grade 10, we didn't get comments on the page, only a percent. My marks showed that this wasn't helping. Without comments, I had no idea what I was doing wrong or what I could do to help it.

Her comments indicate the importance of using rubrics, because they contain descriptive information about the student's writing. It is not helpful to simply assign a mark or grade to a piece of writing. Teacher comments attached to the rubric can also be helpful, according to this student. Paul Black and his colleagues would agree with her observation. Their research with teachers led to suggestions for improving the quality of teachers' comments on student writing so that students could not only understand the teacher's feedback but also use it to improve their writing.

Some teachers indicate that they regularly share with each other the task of assessing writing (known as inter-rater reliability). They ask a colleague to mark several student papers that they have also marked and then discuss the differences in their assessments. This can help teachers recognize that any marking of writing is subjective. It also ensures, for the students' sakes, that their work has been fairly assessed.

STANDARDIZED TESTS

Today, it is understood by teachers, parents, and students alike that achievement tests are here to stay. They are used to encourage an environment of accountability for schools by evaluating student performance. What are the relative merits of standardized tests? Evaluation and assessment experts argue that standardized tests provide educators with a common "yardstick" with which to measure the performance of students, teachers, and schools. Government departments of education have all students in a school district or in a province or state take the test.

Test results determine if students' achievements are meeting standards within subject areas and across geographical areas. This allows educators to make decisions about students, programs, and funding.

Concerns about standardized tests range from worry that they provide a false sense of objectivity and that they diminish certain groups (females, children of colour, children from lower socio-economic levels, and children living in rural areas, for example) to narrowing curriculum demands to easily marked areas. Detractors of standardized tests favour other types of assessments to measure what students do in classrooms on a daily basis.

My concern with standardized tests as they pertain to writing lies in the belief that writing instruction can be simplified to a set of tools and techniques that will automatically produce a satisfactory or good score on a test. While many activities and assignments can help students improve as writers, engaging in these without close attention to the writer and his or her beliefs, experiences, and values will not result in significant long-term results in writing development. This close attention cannot be identified on a standardized test.

Students indicate that they appreciate knowing the categories that are important parts of a good piece of writing. These categories are often specified in standardized tests. Categories may differ somewhat from test to test but, generally speaking, include: vocabulary, sentence structure, organization, content and/or ideas, and mechanics. Teachers can use these categories, perhaps modified, to both assess and evaluate student writing and to prepare them for standardized tests.

There is some fear among educators and writers themselves that an overemphasis on preparing students to do well on a standardized test in writing will have a negative influence on the assessment-for-learning procedures that teachers may have developed throughout the school year. This could happen if teachers abandoned the assessment-of-learning approach in favour of preparing students to write only on specific topics and using only specified forms. Paul Black suggests ways to combat the negative effects on standardized testing. For example, teachers can encourage students to reflect on their learning throughout the year so that, when they do prepare for a standardized test, they know the areas to work on and feel confident in their abilities (that is, an assessment-for-learning approach, not just evaluation). In addition, teachers, parents, and students can work toward understanding the relationship between assessment for learning and standardized evaluation and the value of each. While we believe that assessment for learning should dominate the feedback process in teaching writing, there should be little fear of the standardized test, because it also provides helpful feedback for students, teachers, and administrative personnel.

Ten Writing Assignments

In writing practice we are allowed to express everything about a situation. If we like, we can go on for three pages about how we hate the photo, then skip to the boss who once fired us, then to our aching back, the saltshaker, our true love, the dog we lost. But now we are writing for a reader, and the new taste of responsibility is in our mouth. There is another person here. We have to communicate, get the picture across. How best to get that result? (Goldberg, Thunder 166)

Goal of this Chapter

My goal in this chapter is to help students learn to write for a variety of purposes with a reader in mind. I present 10 writing assignments that can be used in any classroom where students are engaged in writing, not only in language-arts classes but also in other subject areas. These assignments will most likely be successful if students are already writing on a regular basis in their classrooms. The assignments are carefully constructed and presented so that both new and experienced teachers can use them in their own classrooms.

An important characteristic of any writing assignment is defining it and assisting students in their interpretation of it. According to Erika Lindemann, any good writing assignment must take into consideration the teacher's goals and how the students will interpret it, and, I would add, who the readers might be. In designing a writing assignment, teachers need to keep in mind the questions listed below, which the student will eventually need to answer:

- Who is this writing for?
- What do I know about the subject?
- How do I feel about it?
- What is the deadline?
- What form will the writing take?
- What is my purpose?
- What is my personal connection to this assignment?

The 10 writing assignments offered in this chapter were created, implemented, and evaluated by classroom teachers who were experienced in working with teens at the middle- and high-school levels. They designed them after having received feedback from teens themselves, and we know them to be effective. We know that no single writing assignment can appeal to all students, so we encourage teachers to offer choices from among our offerings and to modify them where necessary to best meet their own students' needs and interests.

Each assignment contains:
- the rationale and background
- instructions to the teacher
- a student handout
- examples of student work
- modifications
- assessment and evaluation
- a final consideration

ASSIGNMENT 1: A MODERN FAIRY TALE

Rationale and Background

The modern fairy-tale assignment provides an opportunity for students to create a story, an activity most students still enjoy doing in middle school and high school. Students build upon sometimes-unconscious knowledge of the fairy-tale genre. The first step is for them to decide on a favourite fairy tale to modify. They then add a modern setting, modern characters, and a modern situation. Students receive instruction from the teacher and have the experience of working through The Writing Process with their peers.

My colleague Carrie remembers this assignment when she was in grade 7, and she still has the original version of the modern fairy tale she created. She remembers it as both fun and challenging and often shares it with her students; they appreciate knowing that their teacher is also a writer.

Instructions to the Teacher

1. Introduce the fairy-tale genre by bringing in several well-written retellings. Three excellent examples are: *Frog Prince Continued* (Scieszka), *Goldilocks and the Three Bears* (Marshall) and *Jack and the Beanstalk* (Kellogg). Review with students some elements that are found in many fairy tales and share historical information about the origins of certain fairy tales, including, for example, events from the lives of the Brothers Grimm.
2. Have students list some of their favourite fairy tales and give brief summaries of them, noting similarities and differences among them.
3. Once students have renewed their interest in and general understanding of fairy tales, and have listed a wide variety of these to choose from, distribute the student handout and rubric to share and discuss (see appendix J).

4. Have students choose a group to work with, or they may choose to work alone if they desire. Once students have decided on groups, send them to the library and/or computer lab to choose a specific version of a fairy tale to work with. They hand in the library version with their own final project.

5. Once students have chosen and read their fairy tales from the library, have them brainstorm about how to modernize the story. Suggest that they list the details of the fairy tale on one side of a piece of paper and write ways to modernize those details on the other side. For example, if they are using Hansel and Gretel, they might write the names Hansel and Gretel on one side of the page and Hank and Ginger on the reverse side. They might use a reform-school setting instead of a forest. Have students begin writing a draft and go through all stages of the process.

6. Monitor students' group work during brainstorming, drafting, editing, and publishing.

7. Have students work on a visual representation of an aspect of the fairy tale. Students could draw, generate something from the computer, or cut out magazine pictures that illustrate the storyline of their modernized fairy tale. Tell students to make their projects look like a children's book—for example, they might use cardboard for the cover. Have students present their fairy tales to the entire class or to younger children at other schools.

Student Handout

Once upon a time, in a land not so far away . . . As young children, your minds were filled with images, listening to the classic words of stories passed down through generations: *Cinderella, Sleeping Beauty, Rumplestiltskin, Hansel and Gretel, The Ugly Duckling, The Frog Prince, Puss in Boots*—the list goes on and on. You have likely heard these stories many times.

A new challenge for you, as a writer, is to put a modern-day twist on a classic fairy tale and publish it for younger readers. Choose one of your favourite fairy tales and rewrite it, placing it in today's setting. Change the setting, the names, and the events of the original fairy tale. However, keep the underlying storyline the same. For example, you may want to modernize Hansel and Gretel. Instead of using the names Hansel and Gretel, you might use Hank and Ginger. Instead of the stepmother trying to lose the children in the forest, you might send them away to a private boarding school. Instead of a witch who terrifies the children, you might have the school's lunch monitor play this role. These are just a few suggestions to help you get started on creating your very own version of a fairy tale.

Form a group for working on brainstorming, writing, editing, and illustrating of your story. Groups of two or three students work best. Draft your ideas, provide rough copies, and hand in a piece that others will want to listen to and read. The final product should resemble a children's book in its physical appearance, both inside and out. The storyline could be aimed at students your own age or younger.

Stephanie knew all the stories about the Deziree Sea – she had lived on its shores for all her seven years. She knew about the magical creatures that were said to inhabit the bottom of the sea: mermaids, seahorses, roaring sea lions, the sea monster and, of course, the giant whales. She had heard many stories, but she had never seen the creatures herself.

In her seventh year, terrible events took place at the edge of the Deziree Sea. Fishermen, swimmers, and those who played along the shore disappeared, no one knew where they had gone. The woman who sold apples in the market was gone, the old man who sat in the rocking chair by the sea, even the painter living next door – all were gone, all disappeared.

— Holly, one of the participants in the study, used the story "Pinocchio" as the basis for her modern fairy tale, "Stephanie and the Whale," which she wrote in a grade-12 creative writing class.

Even with news of the disappearances, Stephanie couldn't stay away from the salty water, the sand and never-ending horizon. One day she went swimming, went far out into the ocean, farther than she had ever been before. She swam with the multicolored fish, and all was well. Soon the shore was gone and she was surrounded by only ocean. The waves were getting larger and Stephanie bobbed up and down in the water.

In the distance, Stephanie saw a spray of water, curving and arcing into the air. The spray of water created a rainbow, and Stephanie was still as the spray moved closer and closer. Soon the spray sprinkled water on her face, and then, slowly, a shadow emerged from the water. Before Stephanie could even move, the large head of a giant blue-gray whale rose from the water, its two black eyes staring her directly in the face. The whale opened its mouth and swallowed Stephanie whole.

Here is an outline to guide you:

1. Find a group of two or three classmates to work with. You may work by yourself if you wish, but just know that you will have to do a little more work!
2. Research some fairy tales.
3. Decide on a fairy tale you wish to modernize. Get a copy of the fairy tale to hand in with your assignment and to follow as you create your new version.
4. Outline some of the main ideas of the classic fairy tale. You can do this by making a list of events, characters, settings, and themes.
5. Brainstorm ideas about how to make a modern version of the fairy tale. Decide on a general storyline, the setting, and the characters' names.
6. Draft a rough copy of the story.
7. Edit your story.
8. Produce a published piece of writing.
9. Make your modernized fairy tale look like a children's book. Include illustrations to enhance your story. Try to add texture and vibrant colour.
10. Make your fairy tale stand out and get the attention of a publisher.
11. Have fun!

Modifications

Struggling readers and writers, too (not just exemplary students), are able to enjoy working on this assignment. Find a version of the fairy tale that meets the needs of struggling students to guide their writing. This version would feature detailed illustrations and less sophisticated vocabulary than a version for exemplary students. You might use computer software that helps students read a fairy tale. You can modify the standard rubric by reducing the overall marks or by changing it into a checklist.

Assessment and Evaluation

The modern fairy-tale assignment should be evaluated with a rubric (see appendix). It has a five-point scale that assesses student performance in: (1) thought and detail, (2) creativity, (3) mechanics, (4) diction, and (5) overall impression and effort. The rubric provides descriptive feedback that can help students improve their performance. The group process can be evaluated by the students themselves, and an oral presentation at the end can also be evaluated for participation and effort.

A Final Consideration

Try to devote a few weeks to the modern fairy-tale assignment. Students might ask if they may use a teen storyline and content. The content must be appropriate to the age group for which it is being written. The final product must still look like a children's book and be in keeping with the fairy-tale genre.

ASSIGNMENT 2: A CHARACTER GROWS UP

Rationale and Background

The character-grows-up assignment engages students in a structured form of creative writing. Students reflect upon a character in a book, movie, or play and speculate on his or her life in 10 years. It helps students think about aspects of character development. For example, students might choose to have Ponyboy write a letter to Cherry (characters from S.E. Hinton's novel *The Outsiders*) explaining what his life is like after 10 years have passed. Students would reflect on aspects of the character and, at the same time, engage in the letter-writing form. Students speculate about a character's future actions based on what they already know about him or her after reading the story. This assignment is most suitable for students in grades 7, 8, and 9. However, it can easily be adapted for older students.

Carrie's and my experiences show that students are so interested in the characters and the storyline of *The Outsiders* that they work eagerly. Teachers can encourage students to choose one of many forms for this assignment—for example a journal, letter, story, interview, or descriptive essay.

Instructions to the Teacher

1. Have students participate in a thorough class study of S.E. Hinton's novel *The Outsiders* (or some other novel, play, or movie).
2. Focus on a particular character—what the character says, how the character treats others, what others say about the character, and how others treat the character. Have students talk about how they perceive and react to this character.
3. Focus on specific writing skills—spelling, grammar, sentence structure, word choice. Give them a mini-lesson on sentence analysis.
4. Identify the various forms from which students can choose. The more options students have for their writing, the more interesting and effective their pieces will be.

Student Handout

The novel *The Outsiders* by S.E. Hinton includes many explicit details about its characters. The reader gets to know the characters by taking note of what they say, what other characters say about them, what they do, and how they react to certain events. The reader gets to know what the character looks like, what they are afraid of, what they think about, and what they hope for and dream about.

However, in the novel we learn what the characters are like only at the time the story is occurring (the present) and not what they become after the story ends. Your writing task is to create a descriptive piece focusing on one of the characters from the novel *The Outsiders* and indicate what he or she would be like 10 years after the story takes place.

Choose one of the following characters from *The Outsiders* to write about: Ponyboy Curtis, Darry Curtis, Two-Bit, Sodapop Curtis, Cherry Valance, or Steve. For example, Ponyboy is 14 at the end of the novel, so you will write about what his life would be like at 24.

This is descriptive writing, so provide as much detail as possible. Use information that you have learned from reading the novel. For instance, if you think that Two-Bit is going be in jail in 10 years, that must be apparent from what you already know about this character from reading the novel. What makes you think this? Be very specific. You may choose the format you would like to write in—for example, a paragraph, a story, a letter, a journal, or an interview.

Use the second- or third-person point of view, not the first (i.e., do not use "I," "we," "our"), unless you are pretending to be the character you are writing about. Hand in a rough copy of your writing for feedback at some point during the process. The final copy should be typed and double-spaced.

Some questions to consider are:
- What would that character be doing now?
- Would he/she be married? Divorced? Single?
- Would he/she have children? If so, what type of parent would he/she be?
- What type of job would he/she have? (Would he/she even have a job?)
- Where would he/she live?
- What type of community and home would he/she live in?
- What type of car would he/she drive?
- What would he/she look like?
- How would he/she act?
- Would he/she be the same as he/she was as a teenager, or would something have made him/her change?
- What are his/her friends and family like?

Good Luck!

Modifications

With the character-grows-up assignment, teachers may limit the amount of writing expected for struggling students. The teacher and student can hold a conference in which the student decides which form would best match his or her academic abilities. For instance, reluctant writers may find it more enticing to talk about their ideas first and then write a letter to meet the assignment guidelines. This is because a letter is a more concrete type of writing, which most students know how to do. Teachers can challenge advanced students by asking them to create a multi-level assignment—asking the student to perform the piece for an audience, for example. This works well for students who write in journal form (they can perform it as a monologue) or for those who write in interview form (they can dress up as the character and perform the interview with the help of another student who acts as interviewer).

Assessment and Evaluation

The character-grows-up assignment is best assessed and evaluated with a rubric that includes the following criteria: content and ideas, organization, sentence structure, vocabulary, mechanics, and the

Dear Aunt Laurie and Uncle Kirk,

Twenty-seven years feels like a long time when you're living on a ranch, but if there's one thing I'll never get tired of, it's the happy music of songbirds in the morning. I don't do much except feed and ride the horses. Mickey Mouse is my favourite.

Yeah, I found the legendary Mickey Mouse. I was wandering around at an auction one afternoon and I spotted a sign that read FOR SALE! Pure-bred quarter horse—best offer. Then, I remembered the drive-in movie house, where Ponyboy Curtis first told me about his brother's horse, Mickey Mouse. I didn't think it was very likely that this particular horse could possibly be Mickey, but I took my chances and bought that horse for an entire forty thousand dollars. Mickey is a valuable gelding, and I figured forty grand wouldn't be enough, but it was, by a lot. The highest bid next to mine was twenty-five thousand, so I wish I hadn't spent so much. It was worth it, however.

I rushed to get home, pulling the distraught horse along beside me, hoping to sit down and spend a few hours tracking down Sodapop Curtis. After scribbling down more phone numbers and addresses than I can even express, finally, a name popped up. Marcia Curtis, employee of SAA accounting, 4th Street South, Los Angeles. Nearly dropping the phone, I contacted the operator and asked for the number of a Marcia Curtis.

Just as I had suspected, my long-lost friend Marcia had been happily married to Soda for four years now. I arranged for them to come down to Birmingham and visit for a day or two, and it was immediately decided Friday was the perfect day for a visit in the country.

When Friday finally came, I sprang out of bed to have a shower and brush my rat's nest of red hair. Doing my best to apply makeup evenly on my freckled face, I heard a car drive up. Nearly falling down the stairs, I sprinted to the door to greet Soda and Marcia. At the door, I ran my hands down my new blouse and smacked a smile on my face. "Hi! Long time no see!"

"Hey! Cherry! I haven't seen you for ages!" Marcia laughed and approached to give me a hug. Over coffee, Soda, Marcia and I explained about our lives. After sitting in the living room for about an hour discussing politics, I decided to show them Mickey Mouse.

When Soda saw the horse, he gasped and went over to once again stroke the hair of his lost but not-forgotten friend. Assuming that this horse was indeed the one-and-only Mickey Mouse, I explained to Marcia that I could easily arrange a trailer back to L.A., but when we brought the issue to Soda he insisted I keep Mickey, that I could keep better care of him. I agreed and welcomed them to stay for as long as they wished, but they ended up leaving the next day, something about "family business."

So, here I sit, once again opening cards, and I can't help but wonder, "Is my life going anywhere?" Gently picking up the phone, I dialed the one number I kept on my desk at all times. "Hello? Yes, I'm wondering if I can apply for a job. Yes, I have a degree in teaching . . ."

—A student uses the letter form and writes as the character Cherry (first person) from *The Outsiders*. A poster accompanies this piece; it demonstrates how visual representation can help students express their understanding of a particular character.

improvements made through editing from the first draft to the published copy. The reason to award marks in editing is to show the student's knowledge of and attention to the use of editing and proofreading to improve a piece of writing (see appendix K).

A Final Consideration

The character-grows-up assignment might seem like a lot of writing for reluctant writers. To alleviate this problem, the teacher can spend time, while presenting the novel, play, or film, focusing on character development. Teachers should pose questions about character development and ask students to provide extensive detail. They might find themselves surprised at how much they know about a specific character and can speculate about his or her life in 10 years' time.

ASSIGNMENT 3: A SHAKESPEAREAN SHAKEUP!

Rationale and Background

The Shakespearean-shakeup assignment is a good warm-up activity for a unit on Shakespeare (e.g., *Hamlet, Romeo and Juliet, Macbeth, A Midsummer Night's Dream*). It works best with senior students who have some background knowledge of and exposure to Shakespeare. In the same way that Lois Burdett, author of the popular series Shakespeare Can Be Fun!, brings Shakespearean literature to children by demystifying its language, this assignment helps make Shakespeare accessible to teens. Students can experiment with Elizabethan language and appreciate its beauty.

Instructions to the Teacher

1. Review life in Elizabethan times (end of the 1500s and the early 1600s) and provide information documenting Shakespeare's life and times. This can be done in a variety of ways—from showing excerpts from modern films of the plays, to sharing pictures from books, to reading literature from Shakespeare's time. One great picture book is *A Midsummer Night's Dream* by Bruce Colville. Have students find pictures and descriptions on the Internet to share with the class.

2. Distribute a short handout on Shakespearean language to students. Read a sampling of Shakespeare's works with students—pages from a play, a sonnet, and a soliloquy, for example—to familiarize students with the language and the forms that Shakespeare used. Follow this with a reading from one of the books in Lois Burdett's series in which she and her students have rewritten and illustrated Shakespeare's plays. Show the film documenting Lois's work, entitled *The Secret of Will*, which nicely demonstrates the fun of reading, writing, and performing Shakespearean literature.

3. Have students read a favourite poem. "Eighteen," by Maria Banus is a good choice. Discuss the poem with students and consider its meaning.

> ### Eighteen
>
> Maria Banus
> (translated by Willis Barnstone and Matei Calinescu)
>
> Wet streets. It has rained drops big as silver coins,
> gold in the sun.
> My mind charges the world like a bull.
> Today I am eighteen.
>
> The good rain batters me with crazy thoughts.
> Look. Drops are warm and slow
> as when I was in carriage, pinned tight
> in diapers, drenched and unchanged for an hour.
>
> Yes, it rained as tomorrow, in the past, always.
> The heart scrapes through time, is one heart.
> my temples beat stronger than temples of time.
>
> Like a common bum I think of drinking life,
> but I am burnt, even by the hot stream of its juices.
> I am eighteen.

—A poem used by a teacher to introduce the Shakespearean-shakeup writing assignment (used with permission)

4. Once students demonstrate that they have acquired an understanding of the poem, have them work on recreating it using Shakespearean language. Encourage students to have fun and not feel restricted. Have them work out their ideas, draft a rough copy, and finish with a publishable copy, which they can read aloud to the rest of the class.

5. At the end of the assignment, have students answer the six follow-up questions (listed on page 92) in order to reflect on the assignment, the process, and the work produced.

Student Handout

You are about to embark on a journey, one that often leads you into a dark place in the depths of the unknown, a world that is so different that it leaves you baffled. This place is known as *Shakespearean times*. We are beginning a unit that revolves around some of the classic literature from the 16th century, specifically that penned by William Shakespeare. In order to take some of the fear out of studying this period of time, we are going to have a little fun with Shakespearean language! Together, we are going to read the poem "Eighteen" by Maria Banus. After some careful thought and consideration of this modern poem, you are going to join a partner (or you can tackle this on your own if you so choose) and rewrite it, transforming it into Shakespearean language.

This assignment gives you a chance to explore Shakespeare's writing and allows you a little fun at the same time. The goal is to fabricate your own version of what Shakespeare might have done and to make it sound Shakespearean. After you are done, write a short response to each of the six follow-up questions:

1. Did you enjoy this writing assignment? Why or why not?
2. How do you feel about the piece you produced?
   Is it effective writing? Why?
3. Do you think this was an effective assignment for getting you
   to think about Shakespearean language? Why or why not?
4. Was this a difficult piece of literature to write? Why or why not?
5. What was the best thing about doing this assignment?
6. If you had to give yourself a mark out of 15, based equally
   on your thoughtfulness, creativity, and mechanics, what would
   you give yourself? Why?

Once you have answered the follow-up questions, type up your published copy of the poem and attach your answers to the follow-up questions. Only one copy of the poem needs to be submitted per group, but each of you needs to answer the questions on your own. Then, present your poem to the class. Make it interesting and write in the true spirit of Shakespeare!

Enjoy!

Modifications

The Shakespearean-shakeup assignment works well for students of varying language abilities, because they work together and help one another interpret the poem and rewrite it. If students have difficulty using the poem form, the teacher can suggest rewriting the poem in another way—for example, in letter form, as a journal entry, or as a quick write.

---

1. Yes, we enjoyed this writing assignment. It was a good break from simply reading Shakespeare. It also provided a creative and new way of understanding and studying two different types of literature.

2. We think our poem is fairly effective because it sounded convincingly Shakespearean and generally had a good flow, even though it barely resembles the original piece.

3. Yes, we think this assignment was effective in getting us to think about the Shakespearean language. It made us realize how different writing was in the 16th century than it is today.

4. At first, this assignment looked like it would be easy to write. However, when we actually started, we discovered how "out of place" it felt to change writing from a modern form we are familiar with to one we are not so familiar with.

5. The best thing about doing this assignment was being able to use words like "whore" and "bosom".

6. If we had to give ourselves a mark out of 15 based on thoughtfulness, creativity, and mechanics, we would give ourselves a 14 because we did a good job aside from the fact that it may not have the flow and rhythm the original poem had.

—Three students' responses to the six questions posed after completing the Shakespearean- shakeup assignment

---

XVIII

By Mike, Brandon and Alan

Dank cobblestone. Raindrops as silver coins doth plague the ground,
shimmering in that great celestial orb.
Mine thoughts doth wander hither and thither as a bull charg'th,
This day, the eighteenth anniversary of mine birth doth approach.

Drops thrive in warmth and slothfulness
As whence in carriage I did dwell, pinned firm.
wielding diapers, soiled, stained with urine didst I remain.

Yea, it raineth as always, days past, still to come.
The heart in the bosom grazes through the whore that is time, rendereth one heart.
Mine temples doth surge with more zeal than temples of time.

Like a vile vagabond methinks oft of drinking lire,
But singed and charred am I, even by the scorching stream of the juices to which it doth belong.
Alas mine eighteenth doth come hence.

—A poem created by three grade-12 students in response to the Shakespearean-shakeup assignment

Assessment and Evaluation

For the Shakespearean-shakeup assignment, the teacher gives marks for participation or completion and comments on the students' responses to the questions posed in the student handout rather than on the end product. This lets the students engage in the assignment for the purpose of just playing with language and not focus on meeting a particular standard. Self-evaluation helps the teacher see how the students perceive the writing they have completed and performed. (See self-evaluation in the Student Handout section of this assignment—six follow-up questions—page 92.)

A Final Consideration

Students sometimes balk at completing the follow-up questions, so the teacher needs to give them special encouragement for this aspect. Some students do not like doing assignments when they do not get marks for them; the teacher can give participation or completion marks in such cases. However, grading the Shakespearean-shakeup assignment diminishes its main purpose of helping students learn to enjoy and play with language.

ASSIGNMENT 4: A CHARACTER SKETCH

Rationale and Background

The character-sketch assignment helps students pay attention to characterization as a way of understanding a text, and it can be adapted for various grade levels and genres. It works well for examining characters in movies, novels, and some short stories. Students tend to enjoy literature when they can relate to a certain character. This assignment asks students to choose a character and pay attention to the details of the story that allow them to get to know that character. It also provides a structured format that helps students develop organizational skills: it deals with thesis statements, topic sentences, introductions, and conclusions. It also encourages students to identify effective and thorough development of an idea.

Instructions to the Teacher

1. Discuss the importance of characterization in a piece of text before students read the text. Use this opportunity to talk about the methods that a writer uses to create a character—for example, how the character looks, what the character says, how others react to the character, and what others say about the character. Read from a novel like *Lucas* by Kevin Brooks or *Alice, I Think* by Susan Juby to introduce an interesting and unique character to the students.
2. Once students read the piece of literature or review the movie, have the whole class list and discuss the major characters. Help students understand major and minor characters and identify both flat and dynamic characters.
3. Use lists, charts, and/or Venn diagrams to outline each character and to compare them.
4. Once students understand and appreciate the various characters and their roles in the novel, have them choose one that they can use to develop a character sketch.
5. Discuss the forms that students can use to write the character sketch. Have them draft their ideas about a specific character and then organize their ideas into five main paragraphs. This introduces students to the five-paragraph essay format and at the same time engages them in writing about someone who is of interest to them.

Student Handout

Follow these steps in order to create a magnificent character sketch! Write five paragraphs that contain a sufficient amount of information so that the reader gets to know the character as well as you do. Make it interesting and exciting for the reader, and share your interest in the character!

1. Write an introductory paragraph. It should include:
   - ideas about the piece of literature in which the character "resides"; do this by providing quotes, questions, and/or general statements and observations

- a thesis statement that includes title and author or producer of the piece; identification of the character being sketched; the three main traits that you are going to discuss, in the correct order

2. Write body paragraph #1. It should include:
   - a topic sentence that introduces the first trait listed in the thesis
   - three specific examples from the piece of literature that show how the character displays this trait

3. Write body paragraph #2. It should include:
   - a topic sentence that introduces the second trait listed in the thesis
   - three specific examples from the piece of literature that show how the character displays this trait

4. Write body paragraph #3. It should include:
   - a topic sentence that introduces the third trait listed in the thesis
   - three specific examples from the piece of literature to show how the character displays this trait

5. Write a conclusion. It should include:
   - a restatement of your thesis (from the introduction) in different words (i.e., it should not be exactly the same as previously written)
   - a general statement, in a few sentences, about the character that leaves the reader informed and satisfied that you have portrayed him or her accurately and thoughtfully; make it interesting so that the reader shares your enthusiasm about the character

Remember to use formal writing, and make sure that the editing process is evident. Use a thesaurus to make creative word choices. Add variety to your sentence structure (do not structure all of your sentences in the same way). Create a cover page for your final copy. (Remember to include the title, an illustration that reflects the subject of your character sketch, your name, the class, the teacher's name, and the date.)

Have fun!

Modifications

For students with specific learning difficulties, the character-development assignment can be modified by decreasing the number of character traits and the number of detailed examples supporting each trait. The teacher might incorporate technical support to assist struggling students. Teachers might also engage adult scribes to record a student's oral description of a character. It is helpful to provide students with a chance to engage in conferences and edit in collaboration with the teacher and other students. Teachers can have advanced students draw a picture or create a poster that reflects the character to further exemplify the ideas they have written.

Sorsha from *Willow*

Have you ever wondered what it would be like to be three feet tall your whole life? Willow Ufgood in the movie *Willow* has to live his life like that with all the other Nelwyns. The Brownies are even shorter than Willow. In the movie *Willow*, directed by Ron Howard, Sorsha, who is one of the main characters, is evil and a traitor but then transforms to being compassionate in the end.

During the beginning of the movie, Sorsha shows that she is evil. One way that she is wicked is when she goes after Elora so that her mother can take away her spirits, which would kill her. Another way is that Sorsha took Elora away from Willow so her mother can kill her, then made Madmartigan and Willow slaves. The last time that she was sinful when she kicked Madmartigan in the face because he told her that he was looking at her leg when Sorsha asked him what he was looking at.

Sorsha is a traitor to her mother, Queen Bavmora, near the end. The first way is that she went against her mother when she starts to love Madmartigan, then she went on his side of the war. The second way that she betrayed her mother is that she was against her mother in the battle. The last way is that she took Elora away from her mother so that she wouldn't kill the baby princess.

Sorsha is compassionate at the end because she fell in love with Madmartigan. She started to feel empathy for Elora because the baby was about to be slaughtered. She was helpful to Willow because she helped him on his mission by fighting in the war to save Elora. Sorhsa was extremely friendly to Madmartigan because she turned her back on her own mother to help him.

Ron Howard directs the movie *Willow*, which has Sorsha as one of the main characters, who is evil, a traitor, but then is a compassionate person at the end. Sorsha marries Madmartigan and they raise Elora Danan as their own. Sorsha and Madmartigan combined their differences so they could live in harmony together for the rest of their lives.

—One student's character sketch of Sorsha, a character from the movie *Willow*. It demonstrates how the student understands the development of the character through the film.

Assessment and Evaluation

The character-sketch assignment is best graded with either a checklist or a scoring guide. The teacher and the students should decide together which method is best to create the checklist (see appendices L and M).

A Final Consideration

We have found the character-sketch assignment to be especially worthwhile for middle-school students. The only consideration is that some students might have difficulty following the rigid five-paragraph format. To help with this problem, the teacher can choose a piece of literature or film that contains many engaging characters. Films are sometimes easier for students to write about.

ASSIGNMENT 5: PRODUCT ADVERTISING

Rationale and Background

The product-advertising assignment is a good way to teach students to view advertisements critically and understand the techniques used to persuade an audience. The assignment can be part of a larger unit devoted to media literacy in which students are taught to develop an appreciation for and an understanding of the messages that they receive from television and movies, magazines and newspapers, radio, and the Internet.

Carol Koran, from Catholic Central High School in Lethbridge, Alberta, in her book *Teaching Film as Literature,* encourages teachers to help students become "informed and analytic" viewers of the images and messages that bombard them on a daily basis. This assignment is designed to do that, and it could also be used as an effective and useful introduction to a study of media literacy.

Instructions to the Teacher

1. Begin this activity with a focus on the increasing importance of the media in students' lives and the techniques used in advertising that convey information.
2. Share with students Carol Koran's chart that describes the basics of visual literacy (see figure 6.1). The chart is helpful in comparing the standard elements of literature study with those of visual literature. It is important to note that, just as writers carefully choose from the elements referred to by Carol Koran—colour, shape, lines, music, images, motifs, camera angle, light, sound, movement, and editing—to create effective print communication, filmmakers (directors, designers, and editors), make conscious choices about the elements of visual communication. An understanding of these elements, and the meanings inherent within them, can broaden and deepen one's understanding of film as a literary genre.
3. Information about product-advertising elements is best learned by doing. Therefore, after discussing these with the class, ask students to take advertisements from magazines (which they can pick or you can preselect) and do an advertising analysis.
4. Divide the students into groups of two or three students and have each group choose between six and 10 advertisements. Give them the six analysis questions listed in appendix N.
5. After they have finished their analysis, have the students choose their favourite advertisement (or their strongest analysis) and write a paragraph showing the techniques that were used in the creation of the advertisement that made it either effective or ineffective.
6. Have students present the advertisement and their analysis to the rest of the class. Give them a participation mark for this part of the assignment.
7. Have students create their own effective advertisement for some product that is already on the market.

Basic Elements of Literature	Basic Elements of Visual Media
diction (word choice)	colour
figurative language	shapes, lines, music
symbolism	images, motifs
point of view	camera angle
tone	light, sound, movement
syntax (sentence construction)	editing

Figure 6.1. Carol Koran's chart comparing literary elements and visual elements

Student Handout

You are a top executive at a major marketing firm that works with many big companies that produce extremely popular products (e.g., Nike, Pepsi-Co, Guess). You have been selected to create your own "team duo"—a new and exciting ad for the popular product of your choice. With a partner, you are going to choose the product, one that is already well-known and popular, and create a unique advertisement for it. This will be an attempt to remarket the product, and do it differently. The key is to make it your own.

Incorporate specific ideas about shapes, lines, colour, symbolism, and composition to make your ad effective and marketable. You need to consider the product that you are advertising, the audience that you are targeting, the direct message that you are sending, and the implied (subconscious) message that you are sending. Also, you need to consider the effect that the colours, lines, shapes, and composition contribute to the message and purpose of your ad. Other visual elements (such as contrast, texture, and symbolism) should also be incorporated. Your ad should have a specific tone. Know that format and lettering (size, colour, typeface) are also important.

Try to make your ad realistic. Your ad may be done on the computer, drawn on poster paper, or done in any way that you think would be effective, depending on the "look" that you desire.

You need to hand in a written paragraph explaining the choices that you made and the effect that you were trying to achieve. Therefore, you need to know why you incorporated specific elements and techniques into your ad. Answer the six questions on the assessment sheet (see appendix N).

Good Luck! Be creative in your thoughts and style!

—This is a sample of an advertisement created by two students. The product is a cell phone. The students used their knowledge of how advertisers employ colours, shapes, and lines. Their goal was to appeal to a public desire to go anywhere they wished and still be able be in touch with friends and family.

Modifications

The product-advertising assignment could be modified by reducing the number of ads that students need to analyze before creating their own. It might take students with learning difficulties more time to examine an advertisement, so reducing the number of ads they are asked to analyze would allow them work along with the rest of the class without feeling as though they are falling behind other students. The teacher might model for the entire class how to analyze an advertisement by displaying an enlarged ad on a screen and helping students identify the key components and the techniques used to create it. Teachers can display various examples until the students demonstrate that they understand the nature of ad analysis.

Assessment and Evaluation

The product-advertising assignment, unlike some of the other assignments, asks students to either self-assess or peer-assess the advertisement and its effectiveness (see appendix N).

A Final Consideration

Plagiarism might be a concern in the product-advertising assignment. It would be easy for students to borrow ideas from ads that are already in print or in circulation. The teacher should monitor student progress often during the planning stages and have students show them all their work and ideas. To avoid plagiarism, teachers should have students do this assignment during class time. A warning: students sometimes like to create ads selling alcohol or cigarettes or use the *sex-sells* concept; teachers need to discuss ahead of time what is appropriate or not.

ASSIGNMENT 6: ANALYSIS OF A CHARACTER

Rationale and Background

The purpose of the analysis-of-a-character assignment is to help students identify aspects of their own personalities and physical attributes, which they then apply to characters in literature. At the same time, students learn to identify literary elements such as theme, setting, and symbols, and how they relate to a particular character. Students use writing and visual representation to demonstrate their understanding of character development.

Autobiographical poems are a popular form of writing that teachers can use to help students think about characters, what they look like, their intentions, and their thoughts. At the beginning of the year, teachers could have students create autobiographical poems as a way for students to introduce themselves to the rest of the class. Then, at various times throughout the year, students might write about characters they encounter in literature and in movies using modified versions of their own poems. For this assignment I suggest that students write their poems about the characters in the novel *Lord of the Flies* by William Golding. However, the strategy could be used for any character, old or young, living or dead, fictitious or real.

Instructions to the Teacher

1. Have students read or view the text under study, in this case, *Lord of the Flies* by William Golding.
2. Ask students to keep journals throughout the reading or viewing and make notes and comments about the characters. For example, a high-school student reading *Speak* by Laurie Halse Anderson writes, "I feel so sorry for Melinda. I know why she is not talking to anyone, not her friends or parents or teachers, but I think she would feel better if she could tell them what happened."
3. Introduce the autobiographical-poem form to students and ask them to create a poem depicting the essence of who they are.
4. Have students choose a character from the novel or movie under study and create a poem and then a poster that shows their understanding of that particular person. Students need to be able to choose the character they wish to portray, since different students will identify with different characters. One strength of this assignment is that, although students must use a structured format, they are free to demonstrate their personal understandings in creative ways.

Student Handout

You and a partner are going to create a poem and poster (or some intriguing visual that can be displayed on the wall) based on one of the main characters in the novel *Lord of the Flies*. Choose either Piggy, Ralph, Jack, Roger, or Simon. The poem should reflect the information given in the novel and recorded in your journal.

Create a poster based on your poem. Surround the words with images portraying the ideas in your poem. Consider using symbols that are associated with the character. Use contrast, texture, and colour to enhance your ideas. This is a creative assignment, and uniqueness, creativity, and thoughtfulness are important!

Read and enjoy the following self-portrait:

> Linda—
> Honest, carefree, content, and generous,
> Sister of Fran, Jim, and Elaine,
> Lover of the freshness of spring, the laughter of a child,
>   and the excitement of new green leaves,
> Who feels joy when travelling, loneliness in the dark, and
>   nervousness in the dentist's chair,
> Who needs sunshine, Saturdays, and friends,
> Who gives support, encouragement, and smiles,
> Who fears pain, snakes, and the end of a good book,
> Who would like to see respect for our environment, peace
>   in our families, and better housing for the poor,
> Who lives in a small grey house down on Grover Street.
> —Moore

Note that, in just 11 lines of poetry, Linda has captured the main characteristics that she wants you to know about her.

Examine the structure of the poem and notice any patterns. Follow this format and create your own autobiographical poem.

Line 1. Your first name only, or your nickname
Line 2. Four traits or qualities that describe you (use adjectives)
Line 3. Brother/sister of...(their names)
Line 4. Lover of...(three ideas, groups, people, e.g.)
Line 5. Who feel...(three emotions and when you feel them)
Line 6. Who need...(three items)
Line 7. Who gives...(three items)
Line 8. Who fears...(three items)
Line 9. Who would like to see...(three items)
Line 10. Who lives...(briefly but creatively describe where)
Line 11. Your last name only

Good luck, be creative, and have fun!

Quiet, friendly, generous, and athletic,
Sister of Laura,
Lover of my puppies, my horses, and swimming,
Who feels joy when jumping on the tramp, bored when
Traveling, and nervous when speaking in front of
people,
Who needs border collies, exciting books, and physical
activity,
Who gives encouragement, laughter, and help,
Who fears getting stepped on by a horse, bitten by
poisonous snakes, and living with no electricity,
Who would like to see exotic places, animals treated
as humans, and new animals
Who lives in a green house on the end of brick row.

—An autobiographical poem
written by Kirsten, a grade-7
student, according to a format
provided by her teacher

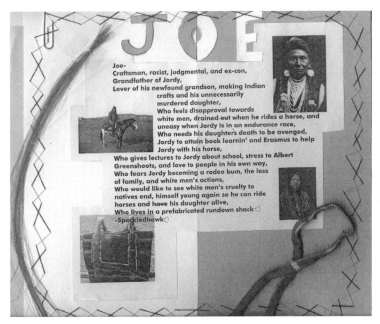

—These samples show the various ways that students can use both writing and visuals to modify
the autobiographical poem that describes Joe, a character from a piece of literature they are reading.

Modifications

Teachers can manage the level of difficulty of a character-analysis project by adjusting the number of students who are allowed to work on it. The more group members there are, the less work there will be for any one student. The visual representation might appeal to certain students and the writing to others, and tasks can be shared accordingly. Teachers might challenge eager students by encouraging them to use a variety of figurative devices, such as metaphors, similes, and alliteration in their writing, or perhaps to create a three-dimensional object to represent the poem.

Assessment and Evaluation

The analysis-of-a-character assignment (poem and poster) is best assessed and evaluated with a rubric that refers to thought and detail, choice, mechanics, and visual representation. The visual representation should be as important as the poem. (See appendix O.)

A Final Consideration

Students generally like the character-analysis assignment, and most of them create very interesting products. As with all group work, teachers need to make sure that the work among group member is equally distributed. Students might benefit from mini-lessons on the use of figurative language. Because this assignment holds wide appeal to students of varying abilities, it is a good opportunity for teachers to uncover and make use of various students' strengths.

ASSIGNMENT 7: STUDYING A NOVEL

Rationale and Background

In this novel-study assignment, Elie Wiesel's novel *Night* is used to teach students to reflect thoughtfully on the themes in a memoir. However, there are other books with compelling content and themes that would do just as well. In this assignment, students learn to recognize such literary devices as symbols, settings, and images that support the major themes of a novel. Students use both writing and visuals to demonstrate their understanding of the novel.

Instructions to the Teacher

1. Have students read the entire memoir before starting this project.
2. During the reading of the memoir, discuss with students the many symbols in it, such as the angel with the sad eyes (representing the slow death of Elie's faith in God), the significance of the time of day (night representing death), the synagogue (symbolic of Elie's faith), and Elie's image of himself in the mirror that looks to him like a corpse (symbolic of both the death of his spirit and the death of his faith). These discussions will help students become aware of the aspects of the memoir that are necessary for this assignment.

3. Provide students with the student handout. Have them brainstorm the important themes that appear in the memoir—for example, loss of faith, loss of innocence or childhood, and overcoming adversity.

4. Have students select their groups (two, three, or four) and have them choose (by brainstorming) the theme they are most interested in exploring.

5. Have students record all of the images, quotes, and symbols in the memoir that relate to the theme they have chosen.

6. Have students decide on a format that will most effectively display their ideas about the theme. Encourage them to present various forms. (Teacher Carrie Netzel has had students build their projects with paper, wood, and steel to depict gallows, synagogues, and prisons, for example.)

Student Handout

After carefully reading and studying the memoir *Night* by Elie Wiesel, you will know more about the subject of the Holocaust and World War II. Your task is to identify one of the major themes of this important piece of literature by discussing images, symbols, settings, and characters. You may do this in groups of two or three or you may do it individually if you wish. The final product should show, in a thoughtful and creative manner, how the theme develops throughout the book and how it affected you as a reader. Use images, colour, texture, text, and contrast to identify the theme you have chosen. Make your work compelling to look at. Originality is important. You must include at least five direct quotes from the book, and do not forget to cite them appropriately.

Think, feel, and work!

Modifications

Most students will be able to participate in this assignment without modification, particularly if the reading of the novel and follow-up discussions have occurred in class. However, for students with learning difficulties, teachers can require fewer quotes from the book. For students who have difficulty with visual representations, teachers can suggest that they explain symbols and images verbally or in writing. To make this assignment more challenging for gifted students, teachers can provide fewer guidelines and allow students to identify a theme in the novel, in both visual and written form, in whatever way they wish (perhaps even perform and/or record it on video).

Assessment and Evaluation

The novel-study assignment, a visual representation in which writing is used throughout the planning and presentation, is best assessed and evaluated with a rubric (see appendix P). The visual component should not be assessed separately from a written component; the visual component should be examined as the product according to the criteria of thought and detail, organization, and choice.

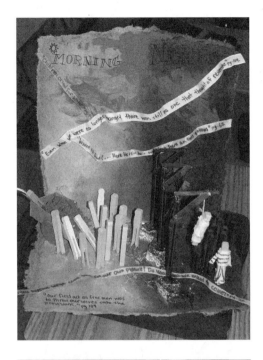

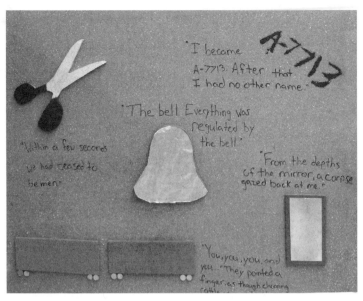

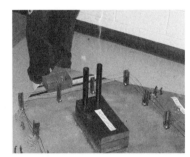

—Students display their interpretations of various themes in the novel *Night* by Elie Wiesel. Note the diversity of their representations.

A Final Consideration

Teachers should have students focus on only one theme for the novel-study assignment. In the memoir *Night,* as in many others, there are multiple themes that are often closely connected. However, students' understanding of the book is strengthened when they focus on a single theme.

ASSIGNMENT 8: A SPECIAL LETTER

Rationale and Background

There are a number of aspects of the special-letter assignment that make it particularly enticing to teens. First, it incorporates the themes of *the future* and *technology* and requires students to use email to communicate with others. This helps students realize how much writing they really do, and how important technology is. Second, it sometimes requires students to view a movie (in this case *The Matrix*). Finally, because the letter is not a typical one, it is unlikely that it will be interpreted as "just another boring writing assignment."

Instructions to the Teacher

1. Provide opportunities for students to read about and discuss the notions of the future and how new technology affects our society. They can do this by reading newspapers and magazines and checking the Internet.
2. Have the class create a Letterman-style top-ten list of either 10 reasons to look forward to the future or 10 reasons to hide from the future.
3. Once you have piqued the class's interest in the future, view the movie *The Matrix*, as a class. This movie uses many "cutting-edge" film techniques and can be used for a film analysis.
4. Discuss with your students the plot of the movie and its characters. Have your students express their viewpoints about how technology affects their lives today and how it might in the future. Then, build on students' ideas by asking about communicating by using a computer.
5. Survey the class to find out how many students use email and MSN, how often they use it, and for what purposes.
6. Distribute the student handout and explain the assignment, indicating that the character Neo in *The Matrix* was first introduced to the "real world" through his computer. Tell the students that they, too, will be communicating with a friend by email.
7. Have students talk with you and with each other so that they thoroughly understand the assignment.
8. Have students work through The Writing Process on this assignment. Engage in conferences with students, both individually and in small groups. Have students email their final copy to you, then email your final feedback to the student.

Student Handout

Pretend that you are living in the time in which the movie *The Matrix* was set. You are Neo (this is your new persona). You are writing an email to a fellow computer-hacker buddy from the "real" world and must explain what has happened to you and what the world is really like, or, more to the point, what is wrong in the world. You are trying to convince your friend that he or she should join you, Morpheus, and the rest of the crew of the Nebuchadnezzar (a strange and futuristic vessel that is their real-world home) in your attempt to help reclaim the planet.

Hey Buddy,

I've been freed! After all my years of searching for the Matrix, I've found the real world. Just as you, I spent my life searching for something I wasn't quite sure existed, thinking my time was almost over. In amidst all of my searching, I had found a world where my life has just begun.

I've met Morpheus, you know, the Morpheus! He found me, yes, after looking so long for him, he's found me. He showed me what the Matrix is, although no one can be told what the Matrix is, all I could tell you is that you're living in a dream world.

The Matrix is a computer system, much like those we've worked on back in the day, but it's not like any other computer system I've ever known. It's an illusion of a world you "live" in, but truly, your body and mind are being kept prisoner here in the real world. Ever since the day we made artificial intelligence, we've been at war with the machines, they imprison us in this dream world so that they can feed off our endless energy source. I know, it's messed up, isn't it?

You should seriously consider knowing the truth yourself and joining us to reclaim the planet. The whole human race that still exists in the real world, I don't know the year, we're all trying to find a way where we can destroy the Matrix and free everyone inside. Buddy, stop living a lie! We plan to unplug as many people as we can from the Matrix and be rid of it forever. Then, everyone will live as some of these natural borns who were born in the city of Zion, they haven't been in the Matrix.

As soon as everybody is free, we will defeat the machines. As of now, there are extraordinary amounts of people living in this fantasy world not knowing they aren't experiencing their life as they perceive they are. I know the truth now, and I am no longer enslaved to the system of false living, you have the same opportunity, Buddy, will you take it? Once we claim our victory over the machines, we can start again and be free forever!

Now I'm going to let you think about it, but the choice is up to you. Do you want to know what the real world is like, or are you going to spend your eternity in that place deep in your mind that it cannot escape unless you join us.

See you soon,
Neo

—A sample of student writing for a particular purpose. Because they have viewed the movie *The Matrix* and taken part in class discussions about the future and technology, the students know enough about a character that they are able to write from that character's point of view.

Convince your friend that people are living pointless lives and are slaves to frighteningly powerful beings who prevent everyone from knowing that they are not in control of their own lives. Except for a few "naturals," who have either been born outside the Matrix or brought out (unplugged), the populous goes about their angst-filled lives, knowing little about how pointless their lives are. Convince your friend that you are one of the lucky ones who have been salvaged and that he or she has the same opportunity. Convince your friend, as well, of the liberating experiences that await him or her and of the chance he or she has to help save the world.

Hey John,

How's it going? Well, I hope you have been doing well and the family is all healthy. I'm pretty good: no complaints. What have you been up to the past few weeks? Do you remember when we were just kids, playing in your backyard all the time, and how we always thought it would be so cool to be able to throw amazing punches or be the best fighter in the universe? Do you remember the pact that we made? It was to make this dream come true before it was our time to pass away. The reason I have brought this memory back to the surface is because I have been given the opportunity to change my life as well as others.

I haven't had a chance to talk to you since I made the choice to take the red pill instead of the blue one. The blue will keep you where you are right now and if you take the red pill you have the chance of a life time to help people realize the real truth in the world. Wait a minute! I'm getting ahead of myself! Now, this all might seem a little strange to you and you're probably very confused; however, promise just to hear me out. When I first arrived (chose the red pill), I was told that I would be "the one" and all I had to do was believe it. "The one" meant that I specifically was chosen to become something more because I had a gift and I could make a difference.

Morpheus, the man who made this all possible, told me that if I believed in this, I could save the world. It took me a while, but Morpheus told me I had to go to this lady and what she had to say would happen because she has yet to be wrong. She told me I was going down the wrong path. Later, I found out that this was just what I wanted to hear, not the truth. Anyways, just because it takes a while to understand it is the truth and it will free you from the slavery, you are in right now as you read this letter.

If you were to join me we can make our childhood dream come to life and you may free your mind from the "not so real" world you are in right now. We are looking for smart, intelligent and bright human beings that are willing to step up to the plate and adventure into the REAL world. I am asking you, as a friend, to come with me on this side so you can experience all the great things I am exposed to. You know I would never lie to you and that I've always wanted the best for you; us being a team would be so beneficial. We have the chemistry that is most needed here.

I hope you understand a little and realize that this will not just alter your life but also make you an even better person. I will be contacting you shortly and I hope by then you've made the right choice.

Your friend,
Neo

—Another sample of student writing for a particluar purpose

This letter needs plenty of detail and description if it is to be effective. Create a name for the friend to whom you are writing and explain how your relationship with this person has come about. Use proper email writing style. Consider your audience and purpose when choosing the language and style.

Please email this assignment to me.

Modifications

The Matrix might be somewhat confusing for students with learning disabilities. For such students, the teacher could clearly review the main

Dear Ms. Martha Stewart,

I am filled with grief as I compose this letter and ponder what I shall write to you. Ms. Stewart, I was utterly devastated when the news reached me of your five month prison sentence. I have watched your television show every day since it started and with you in jail, I do not know what I will do. I absolutely live for your show and your mouth-watering recipes. The fact that they have sent you to jail is an absolute shame and a travesty of justice.

I hope that you are able to pass some of your homemaking skills along to your fellow inmates so that they may gain some of your superior talent. You should also give some advice to the cooks there because I have heard that prison food leaves something to be desired. I also was wondering if they have given you a job so you could have something to do with all your spare time. I think you should take over the decorating for Christmas and try to make it a sublime holiday for each inmate. If you want, I could send you some fabric and you could make a special stocking for each inmate; each could hang one in her cell. Oh, they may not let you have access to a sewing machine or even a needle because it could be used as a weapon. Nonetheless, you are the Queen of Craft and can do miracles with a hot glue gun. In spring, I really hope that they assign you to landscaping because you can do wonders with a few seeds and a shovel, not to mention all the assistance you would have in planting a garden. The prison officials might even let you come back in the fall to harvest the fruits of your labour.

I hope that all is going well and that the other inmates are treating you well in jail. Ms. Stewart, I'm sure that you are enjoying yourself and viewing this as a once-in-a-lifetime opportunity because, as you always say, "It's a good thing." I am already anxiously waiting for your reply.

Sincerely,
Bonnie

P.S. I am hosting a family dinner this year and am hoping you can send me some new exquisite and sumptuous recipes.

—The special-letter assignment can easily be modified for other purposes as well. This example demonstrates a special purpose for writing a letter. It was written by a student to Martha Stewart after news that she would be going to jail. (The letter was not sent!)

ideas in the movie before showing it. Some students might understand the plot and characters of the movie but could have difficulty writing a letter that is meant to convince the reader. The teacher can have these students email a letter to a friend just explaining what Neo has learned or what has happened to him.

Assessment and Evaluation

The special-letter assignment, with its emphasis on communication, is best used as assessment for learning, in which the teacher provides feedback to students in writing and/or in conferences. Students can use this feedback for the final product, which they will share with the class for participation marks only.

Dear Cancer,

My name is Emily and I am nine years old. The doctors say that I am ill because of you. I feel I must write you a letter expressing my anger because I've been told it's not healthy to keep it inside me. I just want to know why you had to choose me.

All I want to do is be a little girl but the doctors say I'm not allowed to go out and play any more because they don't want to chance my condition becoming any worse. My mommy and daddy are always worried and they never let me leave their sight. What did I do wrong to deserve this? My classmates stopped by the other day but they weren't allowed to stay long because the nurse said I needed my rest. It is no fun having you inside me; I just wish that my tummy would stop hurting. I try to yell and scream at you, but you do not hear me. I cry and sob at nights, but you do not listen.

Why do you have to hurt me as well as all the children here? We are all innocent but you have taken that away from us. Do you ever do any good to anyone or are you always there to hurt?

I overheard Mommy say that this is what Grandma had. Grandma isn't here anymore. Am I going to leave too? My mommy, daddy and sister tell me every day how much they love me, and that they are praying for me every day. Do they not think I'm going to get any better?

The doctors came and hooked some more tubes up to me today. There is one through my nose that they say is helping me breathe better because I had troubles last night. I made a friend the other day too, her name is Erica, but the nurses wheeled her off this morning before I woke up and I haven't seen her all day. I wonder if she will be back because she was fun to talk to. There is also Tim across the room from me; he makes me laugh a lot, but he says that you are in him too. They poke and prod and do tests every day I cry out, but they say no one can do anything to stop you. They say that you are in my intestines, I'm not sure what those are but all I know is I'm not allowed to eat anything yummy any more.

Can you just leave? Please? I asked nicely because Mommy always says you get further in life if you are polite. I feel very cold right now and the blankets don't help at all. The coldness is taking over my whole body.

I shall have to go now, Cancer, for I can barely write from the blinding light that is in my eyes. Can you promise me one thing? Don't hurt any others. Just let them be. I don't want them to be cold like I am. Please, Cancer, just let them be. Good-bye Cancer.

Emily

—Here is another letter written for a special purpose. It was written by a student in high school who took on the persona of a 9-year-old living with cancer.

A Final Consideration

Students are often quite intrigued by the idea of emailing their work to the teacher for feedback. They might be less inclined to make changes to their writing if it is not going to be graded. Teachers should stress that the final audience for their writing is their peers. When there is a real audience for their writing, students are more likely to take the teacher's feedback seriously than when there is not.

ASSIGNMENT 9: WATCHING A MOVIE

Rationale and Background

Students today are exposed to a variety of media—video games, television, movies, the Internet, music videos, and computer games, to name just a few. Their ability to interpret these types of communication is referred to as *visual literacy*; it is fast becoming an important and necessary skill. This movie-watching assignment can be adapted for use with a variety of viewing experiences, most notably movies. Have students watch a movie about an important historical or present-day event and write a considered response in the form of an essay. It could be viewed as part of either the English language-arts or the social-studies curriculum. The movie must be interesting and compelling enough to inspire students to write something about it and its effect on them and on society. We suggest *Bowling for Columbine* or *Swing Kids*.

It is important that students have already done the character-sketch assignment before doing this one; they will have been introduced to the essay format. I would suggest, however, that the formal essay form be used only as guide for this assignment; too much structure might inhibit the students.

Instructions to the Teacher

1. Set out for students the purpose for showing the movie. Both *Bowling for Columbine* and *Swing Kids* can be analyzed according to their themes and/or social significance. Both are appropriate for English language-arts and social-studies curriculums.
2. Discuss with students the theme of individuality versus conformity.
3. As your students view the movie, provide each of them with a piece of paper divided into two columns. Ask them to write Individuality at the top of one side page and Conformity on the other. Have them record ideas from the movie that support each of these aspects.
4. When the movie is over, arrange the students in pairs or in threes and have them begin expanding the ideas they have jotted down. Provide each student with a worksheet to help them use writing to clarify their thinking (see appendix Q).
5. Ask students to present their understanding of the movie and its themes in an essay. The two main purposes of this assignment are (1) to help students relate the themes of movie to society and (2) to provide practice in essay writing.

Student Handout

Swing Kids (1993) is the story of a group of teens in Nazi Germany who like to listen and dance to banned swing music from the United States. As the atrocities of World War II unfold, the members of the dance group must face difficult choices about their friendships, about justice, and about survival itself. The characters in the story must confront ideas that cause conflict.

Swing Kids: A Story of Two Friends

by Kirsten

Swing Kids is the story of two young men living in Germany in the days leading up to World War II. The young men, Peter and Thomas, are friends living under the Nazi regime. Although neither of them are Jewish, both of their lives are profoundly affected by the Nazi regime in Germany. Peter's father was arrested for being a Jewish sympathizer, and died shortly after returning from prison. His mother now works in a Nazi factory in order to support her family. They struggle to get by with little resources, living largely at the mercy of the local Nazi block supervisor. Peter's mother is too fearful to speak out against the Nazis in any way, and encourages Peter to "go along" in order to ensure their safety. Thomas' life is very different from Peter's. His family is very rich, and he has all of the means to live quite comfortably. His father, in contrast to Peter's mother, disagrees with Hitler, especially Hitler's foreign policies. He speaks out frequently against the Nazi rule, despite the fact that he had voted for them in the election. Although Peter and Thomas are best friends, throughout the course of the film they each take very different positions in reaction to the rule of the Nazi party in Germany.

Thomas sees the Nazis in power as something over which he has no control. He is extremely idealistic, in that he sees that everyone should be able to have their cake and eat it too. He joins the HJ (Hitler Youth movement) so that Peter, who is required to join, will not have to do so alone. He sees it as the ideal situation: "HJ by day, Swing Kid by night." He sees no reason why they should not take advantage of the many benefits offered by the group protection of the HJ. He enjoys the fact that as a member of the HJ, he has incredible power in the community. He is permitted to go anywhere he likes, receives respect and submission from those around him, and also has access to goods which others did not (e.g., a bicycle). So at first, being part of the HJ was simply a means to a better life, and he took advantage of the system. As he becomes increasingly accepted by the young men in the HJ, and is encouraged and rewarded for his progress, an interesting attitude shift occurs. He begins to believe what he is being told, even to the point of turning in his own father. He becomes so caught up in the fanaticism of the movement that he loses sight of who his real friends are. It is not long before he is completely loyal to the Third Reich, relishing the acceptance and order that he finds there. He goes along on an assignment to close down a swing club, where he had been dancing only a few months before. Here he confronts Peter and, carried away with his loyalty to the Third Reich, he fights Peter, nearly killing him. This is the turning point, and all of a sudden, his eyes are opened. He suddenly realizes that he has turned against his own best friend. Although his position is not explored further (because the movie ends), he salutes Peter with the Swing Kid salute (Swing Heil), which indicates that perhaps at the very end of the movie, Thomas realizes that absolute loyalty to the Third Reich is very dangerous and divisive, and that he could no longer give that kind of loyalty.

Peter's reaction was quite different from Thomas'. Peter's father had died as a result of his outspokenness against the Nazi regime. Peter could not understand why his father had taken such a dangerous position, and felt that surely if the Jews were being punished, they must have done something wrong. It appears, however, that Peter was in denial, and that deep inside, he knew that the Jews had done nothing wrong, had done nothing to deserve the treatment they received. He tries to go along with the regime, in order to make things easier on his family, but is unable to betray his employer, the bookkeeper, and

▶ *continued on following page*

continued from previous page

expose to prosecution actions which he knows are right. Eventually, he realizes that by participating in the Nazi regime, as a member of the HJ, he is helping the Nazis. The suicide of his handicapped friend, Arvid, and the realization that he had delivered to families the ashes of their loved ones, brings the matter sharply into focus in his mind. He abhors the Nazis and everything they stand for. He begins to respect and love his father for his brave actions, and he comes to realize that he too must take a stand. He realizes that if the people of Germany only hear one voice, that of the Nazi party, they will never have the courage to fight the regime. He understands that each person has a moral and social obligation to raise their voice in protest, protecting not only their individual freedom, but the freedom of the individuals around them, especially the ones who are unable to raise their voices in their own defence. After he and Thomas fight outside of the club at the end of the movie, he does not run, but asserts his position on the side of individuality, and is taken away to a work camp.

Although the movie does not have a happy ending, it is a fascinating glimpse into pre-World-War-II Germany. Many people forget that everyone in Germany had to deal with the Nazi rule, whether or not they admitted it. In their own way, each person was forced to deal with the reality of the regime and take their own position in reaction to it. The movie *Swing Kids* illustrates clearly various positions taken by people at that time, in particular two young friends, Peter and Thomas.

—An essay written by a student after viewing *Swing Kids*. The student nicely summarizes the plot and provides the main details of the movie. More important, she identifies the movie's theme—how certain individuals reacted to Nazi rule in pre-World-War-II Germany.

For this assignment, you are to write an essay about the struggles of these teens, particularly in terms of conformity and individuality. The essay should include a summary of the plot and a statement of the social, historical, and political messages of the movie. Ask yourself what, if anything, the movie suggests about the future.

Good luck! Always remember to reread aloud what you have written!

Modifications

For students with learning difficulties, teachers might adjust the length of the essay required. Or teachers might arrange for another person to act as a scribe for a challenged student.

Assessment and Evaluation

The essay in the movie-watching assignment is best assessed and evaluated with a rubric that includes the criteria of thought and detail, choice, and mechanics (see appendix R). Because students need to learn that the content and ideas of an essay are the most important aspects, the first two criteria are worth more marks than is the criterion of mechanics. This is not to say that attention to spelling, grammar, and punctuation are unimportant. The mechanics of writing cannot be overlooked. However, they must be examined in the context of the overall meaning of the piece.

William Lyon Mackenzie King	
1. Birth information	1. December 17, 1874
2. Major accomplishments	2. old-age pension; World War II; national unity

Figure 6.2. An example of a two-column note page that can be used for research

A Final Consideration

Generally, students produce very fine essays about the theme of *Swing Kids* and its effect on them. The teacher should spend time monitoring students' notes and discussions throughout the movie and emphasize that the students will be writing an essay about it. The essay should focus on the importance of the movie's main message.

ASSIGNMENT 10: CONDUCTING AN INTERVIEW

Rationale and Background

In the conducting-an-interview assignment, students connect with Canadian history by "interviewing" a key historical figure. Students conduct research, role-play, and present fictitious, yet believable, interviews and are encouraged to use all the language-arts strands. This assignment helps students meet both English language-arts- and social-studies-curriculum objectives and could be presented in either course.

Instructions to the Teacher

1. To introduce important figures from Canadian history, read an excerpt from Joy Kogawa's novel *Obasan*. This choice will help students recognize that many important and influential Canadian historical figures are still alive. Hand out the evaluation criteria listed in appendix S.
2. Have students work individually or in pairs and have them examine books, websites, class notes (from social studies, for example), newspapers, magazines, and videos to choose a Canadian historical figure and begin their research.
3. Show students how to use a two-column note page to organize their research (figure 6.2). Have them record a word or phrase that refers to the person they are researching on one side of the page and an expanded discussion of that word or phrase on the other side.
4. Have students place their research notes in interview form. Make sure that they refer to the evaluation criteria as they do this (see appendix S).
5. Give students class time to practise role-playing their interviews and to gather props. Have them perform their interviews in front of the class.

Interview with Emily Carr

Ladies and gentlemen, I introduce to you Emily Carr. Emily Carr was born in Victoria, British Columbia, in 1871. She was the fifth daughter of English parents. Both her parents died when she was in her teens, and her older sister Edith took over the household. Emily Carr is becoming famous for her paintings of Canada's west coast and Native culture. She is now 66. Miss Carr, thank you for giving us this opportunity to get to know you a little bit. What did you draw during your childhood, Miss Carr?

My first subject was Carlow, our dog. I sat down beside his kennel and stared at him for a long time. Then I took charcoal and drew him on a brown-paper sack. Soon after, I started art lessons. Two years later, a Victoria tombstone-maker got some plasters of noses, hands, lips and eyes, to help him model angels for his tombstones. I heard that drawing from casts was the way they learned at art schools, so I saved my pocket money and bought some over-size human features. Then I drew them over and over again.

What did you do when you finished school?

I went to study art at the California School of Design in San Francisco. It was the closest art school. There were rats in the drawing hall, and a skeleton haunted the upstairs, but the criticism improved my work. When I returned after three years, I turned the loft of our cow barn into an art studio and gave drawing and painting lessons to children.

Which style of painting did you adopt after your return?

I used a realistic style.

What subjects did you sketch and paint in those days?

Mostly the huge forests near my house. Then a missionary invited me to come to Ucluelet and the West Coast Mission. So, I spent the summer of 1898 sketching the Natives, and their totem poles and canoes.

What did you think of the Native way of life?

Oh, I admired it. Definitely. The Natives didn't fight or try to tame nature. They were also honest about their feelings. When they were sad, they cried, when they were happy, they laughed. The people of Ucluelet were friendly, and nicknamed me Klee Wyck. It means Laughing One.

How did you feel about working near home?

I liked it—living near enough to paint the Native villages. Then, I met several visiting European artists. They told me the only place to learn to paint was Paris or London. They also grandly told me—well "informed" is a better word—that Canada's west-coast scenery was "unpaintable." I guess they were frightened by Canada's vast size. I hoped that studying abroad would help me find the way to paint the beauty of the west coast. So I saved up to study in England, and went in 1899.

Did you accomplish your goal while in England, Miss Carr?

No. When I sailed for home, I felt the five years had been a waste of time. And I hated London. The parks were so tame. They all had prim signs that read PLEASE DO NOT WALK ON THE GRASS or PLEASE DO NOT WHISTLE, SING, OR SHOUT. But I did learn to smoke from my friends.

Did you ever think of getting married?

Well, while I was in England, Martyn, a long-time friend, came from Victoria. He proposed to me again and again. But I wanted to continue my studies. And art was my love.

▶ *continued on following page*

---

continued from previous page

What did you paint after your return?
I took my sketch sack, my food, and Ginger Pop, my dog, and traveled in a small gas-powered boat to the Native villages. I once traded all my clothes except the ones I was wearing for beautiful native baskets. I painted on a small easel surrounded by mosquitoes. I decided to record the art of the totem pole before it vanished. Understanding their art altered my life.

How did it alter your life, Miss Carr?
Well, their wooden carvings showed their feelings about the animal being carved. They weren't trying to show how the animal looked in nature, but to show its fierceness or its grace, or its cunning. The Natives sometimes twisted or altered the shapes to show these deeper meanings. Their art showed essentials, like the part of the beaver that would still be beaver if he was skinned—his energy and his courage, not the insignificant animal on our national emblem. I felt this was the key to capturing the power of the west coast.

Did you start painting the west coast, then?
No. I didn't know how to capture those powerful feelings on canvas.

—An excerpt from one student's fictitious interview with Emily Carr

6. Video-record the interviews to make the situation resemble a television interview and so that students can watch their performances and comment on what they learned by doing the assignment. Have students hand in to you a paper copy of the interview.

Modifications

The most important modification that might be needed for this assignment is to help students find an appropriate figure to interview. Teachers should encourage students to choose a figure from an specific area that interests them—such as sports, the arts, politics, culture, or literature. When students are interested in (even passionate about) a topic, they are more likely to spend the time necessary to research, write, and perform effectively than if the topic does not interest them.

Another way to modify the assignment is to decrease the number of questions the students need to ask during the interview. This shortens the assignment for students who require more time than others to organize and write up their interviews.

Assessment and Evaluation

I would suggest that teachers evaluate interviews using a Likert scale, which allows students to compare their perceptions of how well they did the assignment with those of the teacher. This type of assessment and evaluation procedure gives teachers insight into the learners' points of view as they observe of their own work (see appendix S).

The following are some comments that students made in self-assessing their interviews with Canadian historical figures:
- It was a good activity but stressful for those who do not enjoy public speaking, though I think I improved on this.

Interview with a Grandfather

Welcome to Biography. I'm your host, Amanda Post. Joining us today is my grandfather. Good morning. Please tell us a little about yourself.
I am _____, and a great grandpa, but you can call me Pop. I was born in Japan. I moved to West Vancouver in 1911 to work on a fish boat.

Why did you move to Canada?
I was the youngest son in my family. The oldest son stays home and looks after the parents and the farm. The younger sons were forced to leave. I heard Canada was a land of wealth, much more promising than Japan. So I moved. It was a big risk I took, but I loved fishing, so it was good.

Can you tell us about the events regarding Japanese-Canadians at the beginning of World War II?
All Japanese-Canadians had to register. They had to carry a card with a thumbprint and a photo. Then in December of 1941, the government impounded my fishing boat along with 1200 others. They closed the Japanese newspapers and the schools.

What happened after the bombing of Pearl Harbor during World War II?
The Canadian government passed the "Order in Council PC 1486," expanding the power of the Minister of Justice to remove any and all persons from a designated protected zone (a 100-mile radius of the B.C. coast). This was part of the War Measures Act. On March 4, 1942, I was relocated with about 12 000 others to an internment camp.

What was it like?
Ten family members had to share one stove. Some had to stay in tents because there were not enough houses. The houses had no insulation and it was very cold in the winter. We were everything we had.

What happened to your possessions?
The Government auctioned everything off. They sold everything we had: car, boat, clothes, house. We got no money from the sale of our property, and were never asked if we wanted to sell.

What options did you have after the war?
We could go back to Japan, or move east, but we were not allowed to go back home.

What did you do after the war?
I moved to a small community and began to farm.

Are you happy you moved to Canada?
Yes. My children are not Japanese-Canadian, they are Canadian-Japanese. They were born in Canada; therefore they are Canadian.

—An excerpt from an interview conducted with the grandfather of a student (this one is not fictitious)

- It was interesting to find out more about a figure's personal life instead of just what you read in textbooks.
- I was nervous, and I waved my arms when I was talking. In reality, Emily Carr was very forthright and down to earth, and I don't know if my interview showed that.
- This was a good assignment, because we were able to learn more about who these people in history really were.

- This assignment challenged us to pick an interesting Canadian historical figure. We underestimated how hard it was to act in front of a camera. It was a great experience!

A Final Consideration

Some students are frightened about the prospect of being video taped and performing in front of others. Preparation is key to helping them deal with stage fright. The teacher could have students practise ahead of time in front of a very small audience.

Appendices

Brainstorming Map

Topic

K-W-L-S Chart

Topic: _____

K	W	L	S
What do I know?	What do I want to know?	What have I learned?	What do I still want to know?

Three-Column Revision Checklist

Sentence Beginnings	Sentence Lengths	Verbs

Conference Summary (Narrative Writing)

Writer's Name _____

Critic's Name _____

Title of the Piece _____

Date of Conference _____

The critic should answer the following questions for the writer during the conference and use as much detail as possible.

1. What made the story interesting?

2. Who were the characters? What did you learn about them?

3. How was the setting described?

4. Was the ending what you expected?

5. What did you like best about the story?

6. What was the most exciting part of the story?

7. What part of the story did you want to know more about?

8. What vivid vocabulary or memorable phrases did you like?

Conference Summary (Expository Writing)

Writer's Name _____

Critic's Name _____

Title of the Piece _____

Date of Conference _____

The critic should answer the following questions for the writer during the conference and use as much detail as possible.

1. What have I learned about this topic?

2. What still puzzles me about this topic? What questions do I have for the writer?

3. What is the best line of the piece? Why?

4. How successful was the writer in engaging me as a reader?

Peer-Editing and Self-Editing

The editor asks the following questions (RAFT) to help the writer begin to understand his or her work. The editor should ask these questions before reading the piece and make brief notes of the writer's responses.

ROLE: What role or voice did you adopt in this piece? How did this influence your writing?

AUDIENCE: To what audience is this piece addressed? What concessions did you make to appeal to the audience?

FORM: What form did you choose for this piece? What particular conventions did you incorporate?

TONE: What attitude did you wish to convey about your topic? How did your stylistic choices convey this tone?

Date _____

Title of Piece _____

Name _____

Things I Can Do as a Writer

About thought and detail I can:

About organization I can:

About choice I can:

About convention I can:

Conference Guide

Student's Name _____

Date _____

1. When you read over the comments on your paper, did you have any questions? If so, please write them here.

2. Is there something you would like me to know about your work on this paper?

3. If you had this assignment to do over, what changes would you make?

4. Based on the feedback you received and your mark on this assignment, what would you like me to help you with in your writing?

Rubric for Writing Notebooks

Student Name _____

Three Points: Excellent

1. Used writing not just to demonstrate learning but also as a way to learn.
2. Wrote 250 words or more a week.
3. Used expressive writing.
4. Included questions, ideas, notes, stories, and poems.
5. Experimented with different forms of writing: poetry, fiction, narrative, personal essay, thumbnail sketches, stream-of-consciousness writing.
6. Submitted work in a timely manner, according to class schedule, or made arrangements made with teacher.

Two Points: Satisfactory

1. Used writing to demonstrate learning or as a way to learn (but not both).
2. Wrote regularly but did not submit the equivalent of 250 words a week.
3. Used some expressive writing.
4. Included some questions, ideas, notes, stories, poems.
5. Tried several genres.
6. Submitted notebook three times during the semester.

One Point: Needs Attention

1. Writing did not demonstrate learning.
2. Wrote irregularly and submitted far fewer than 250 words a week.
3. Used little expressive writing.
4. Included few questions, ideas, notes, stories, poems.
5. Wrote in a single voice, style, and genre.
6. Submitted notebook only one or two times during the semester.

A Modern Fairy Tale

Thought and Detail (x 2)

5   Ideas are insightful. This fairy tale would be excellent for children to listen to or read, and you have put a touch of brilliance into your project! You have included many interesting and useful details and a thorough description. You have followed the general storyline to perfection. Way to go!

4   Ideas are thoughtful and interesting. This would be great for children to listen to or read. You have included many specific details and descriptions. You have followed the storyline very well. Good job!

3   Ideas are general rather than specific. Some children might like this story, but it is a little confusing or inappropriate at times. You need to include more detail and description in certain points of the story. You have strayed from the general storyline somewhat. Good attempt!

2   Ideas are vague at times. This would be confusing; it lacks too much information for a child to listen to or read. You need to be much more specific in your details. Some of your ideas just don't fit with the general storyline. A little more work is needed here!

1   Ideas are ineffective or not present. Children would not be able to understand much of the story. Few details were added and the story is too short to be effective. You do not focus on the general storyline enough! A lot more work is needed here!

Creativity (x 2)

5   This looks fabulous! Your illustrations/pictures are creative, attract attention, and fit perfectly with the fairy tale in their design, layout, and quality! Pictures are plentiful and truly make the book a hit! Children will love this!

4   This looks great! Your illustrations/pictures are thoughtful and interesting. They complement the fairy tale in their design, layout, and quality. You have many pictures that add to your book! Kids will find this interesting.

3   This looks fine! You put some effort into your illustrations/pictures, but they could represent the fairy tale a little more. Sometimes the pictures don't seem connected to the story, or they are not consistent throughout the book. Some pictures enhance the book, others don't. Some kids will like it, others won't!

2   This isn't going to be a big hit! You need to jazz up your illustrations/pictures a lot more if you want children to be interested in your fairy tale! Your pictures do not represent the fairy tale well and are inconsistent or irrelevant for the most part. You need to include more pictures to contribute to the book. Most kids wouldn't take a second look!

1   This won't sell a copy! Either you don't have a sufficient number of pictures or they are inappropriate, irrelevant, or lack connection to the fairy tale. Much more work needs to go into this to get a child to read this book!

APPENDIX J

Mechanics (x2)

5   Virtually an error-free fairy tale. The few minor mistakes do not take away from the overall quality of the fairy tale. Excellent writing skills!

4   Errors are minimal. A strong display of writing skills.

3   Errors are present and hinder the quality of the fairy tale at times. Good effort.

2   Errors are too plentiful. Errors hinder understanding on many occasions. Needs more attention.

1   Errors are too abundant and totally take away from the understanding of the fairy tale. You really need to get some extra help with your writing skills.

Vocabulary (Diction)

5   Word choice is creative and strong; it enhances the fairy tale and makes it extremely effective.

4   Word choice is thoughtful and effective on many occasions.

3   Word choice is general rather than specific.

2   Word choice is too general and lacks thought. Words are used incorrectly on occasion.

1   Word choice is non-creative and ineffective. Words are used incorrectly.

Overall Impressions and Effort

5   You have worked extremely hard throughout this entire project! Your project rocks— it is well-written, creative, and a wonderful visual specimen!

4   You have really done a lot of work on this project! It is interesting to read, you have minimal mistakes, and it looks great!

3   You have been working fairly consistently on your project. You need to spend more time proofreading and going that extra mile to make your project stand out. It has some interesting aspects, but most areas are just satisfactory.

2   Your effort has been inconsistent throughout the project and often off-task. You need to edit and put more effort into the creativity of your book. You need to enhance your project on all levels!

1   You have really dragged your feet throughout the entire process. You had difficulty staying on-task, and your book is a reflection of your lack of attention and effort!

TOTAL: ____ /40 = ____%

Comments:

A Character Grows Up

Content and Ideas (x 2)

5   Ideas are effective and well-supported. Assignment is very interesting and extremely detailed.

4   You have quite a bit to say about the character, and the description is well-focused. Assignment is well-supported and interesting.

3   Ideas are evident, but a little more support is needed. Use more specific details and examples.

2   Add more details. Your ideas are not supported by evidence.

1   The reader doesn't know what you mean to say. Purpose is unclear and perhaps off-topic.

Organization

5   Focus is clear and sustained throughout. Strong introductory and concluding sentences/ paragraphs. Ideas are purposefully arranged and effective.

4   This piece has a logical order, and the reader can follow your ideas. Topic and concluding sentences are present and on-topic.

3   Focus is established and generally maintained. Topic sentence could be more specific, but it is sufficient. Ideas stray from the topic the odd time. Sufficient closure.

2   Some parts of this piece are not on-topic. Topic sentence and ideas need to be more focused.

1   Ideas are rarely focused. Topic sentence is not present. Closure falters. The reader would get lost, because there is little focus.

Sentences

5   Good variety of length and type. Purposefully chosen sentences contribute to effectiveness of writing.

4   Sentences are clear, with some attempt to vary length and style. Easy to read.

3   Most sentences are straightforward and basic, easy to read. More variation of length and style is needed. Some sentences are awkward.

2   Problems with run-ons and/or sentence fragments. Sentences are often awkward. More focus needed on sentence length and style.

1   Choppy, short sentences. Very little attention to sentence structure. Difficult to read, because the sentences disrupt the flow of thoughts.

Vocabulary (Diction)

5   Sophisticated and purposefully chosen words add to writing. Words are used correctly and thoughtfully.

4   Words are precise and well-chosen most of the time. There is an attempt to enhance ideas through words.

3   Some evidence of precise and well-chosen vocabulary. Words may not be effective or used properly at times. Some thought given to word choice, but fairly general.

2   Little thought given to word choice. Words are too general and are often ineffective or used incorrectly.

1   No effort given to word choice or how to use words correctly. Word choice hinders reader's understanding of the writing.

Mechanics

5   Very few or no errors. A publishable piece of writing. Superbly written.

4   Very few errors. The few errors present have little effect on the clarity of the writing. Well-written.

3   A few problems with spelling, punctuation, and capitalization. Proofread your paper more carefully. Satisfactorily written.

2   Quite a few problems with spelling, punctuation, and capitalization. Errors make the writing difficult to understand. Editing needs more attention. Weakly written.

1   Problems with spelling, punctuation, and capitalization very abundant and make your work hard to read. Editing must improve. Poorly written.

Rough Copy

5   Editing is evident and greatly enhances the good copy. Attention has been given to all aspects of writing.

4   Editing has been given attention and quite noticeably improves upon the good copy in most areas.

3   Proofreading is evident, but the piece lacks careful examination. Overall result is somewhat improved in some areas.

2   Little evidence of proofreading, and it does not enhance the good copy very much.

1   No evidence of a rough copy or of editing.

TOTAL: _____ /35 = _____%

Comments:

A Character Sketch (Scoring Guide)

Content and Ideas (x 2)

5   Ideas are effective and well-supported. Assignment is very interesting and extremely detailed.

4   You have quite a bit to say, and the piece is well-focused. Assignment is well-supported and interesting.

3   Ideas are evident, but a little more support is needed. Use more specific details and examples.

2   Add more details. Your ideas are not supported by evidence.

1   The reader doesn't know what you mean to say. Purpose is unclear and perhaps off-topic.

Organization (x 1.5)

5   Focus is clear and sustained throughout. Strong introductions and conclusions. Ideas are purposefully arranged and effective. Thesis is effective.

4   This piece has a logical order, and the reader can follow your ideas. Thesis, topic sentences, and concluding sentences are present and on-topic.

3   Focus is established and generally maintained. Thesis and/or topic sentences could be more specific, but they are sufficient. Ideas stray from the topic the odd time. Sufficient closure.

2   Some parts of this piece are not on-topic. Thesis or and topic sentences need to be more focused. Weak conclusion.

1   Ideas are rarely focused. Thesis and topic sentences are not present. Closure falters. The reader would get lost because there is little focus.

Mechanics (x 1.5)

5   Very few or no errors. A publishable piece of writing. Superbly written.

4   Very few errors. The errors present have little effect on the clarity of the writing. Well-written.

3   A few problems with spelling, punctuation, and capitalization. Proofread your paper more carefully. Satisfactorily written.

2   Quite a few problems with spelling, punctuation, and capitalization. Errors make the writing difficult to understand. Editing needs more attention. Weakly written.

1   Problems with spelling, punctuation, and capitalization very abundant and make your work hard to read. Editing must improve. Writing needs greater attention.

Vocabulary (Diction)

5   Sophisticated and purposefully chosen words add to effectivness of writing. Words are used correctly and thoughtfully.

4   Words are precise and well-chosen most of the time. An attempt to enhance ideas through words is evident.

3   Some evidence of precise and well-chosen vocabulary. Words may not be effective or used properly at times. Some thought given to word choice, but fairly general.

2   Little thought given to word choice. Words are too general and are often ineffective or used incorrectly.

1   No effort given to word choice or how to use words correctly. Word choice hinders reader's understanding of the writing.

TOTAL: _____ /30 = _____%

Comments:

A Character Sketch (Checklist)

_____ /2   Attention-grabbing, and interesting introduction is present.

_____ /3   Thesis statement is clearly stated. All three character traits are defined, and the name of the character is given.

_____ /2   Topic sentence #1 clearly identifies the first trait listed in your thesis.

_____ /6   There are three details that describe the character trait in topic sentence #1. Detailed examples from the source are used.

_____ /2   Topic sentence #2 clearly identifies the second trait listed in your thesis.

_____ /6   There are three details that describe the character trait in topic sentence #2. Detailed examples from the source are used.

_____ /2   Topic sentence #3 clearly identifies the third trait listed in your thesis.

_____ /6   There are three details that describe the character trait in topic sentence #3. Detailed examples from the source are used.

_____ /2   The thesis statement is repeated in different words.

_____ /2   Interesting conclusion.

_____ /2   Cover page done correctly and creatively.

_____ /5   Creative use of sentence structure and variation. Careful selection of descriptive words, effective diction and varied sentence composition.

_____ /5   Strong evidence of close proofreading and editing. Ideas are not hindered by mechanical errors. This is virtually an error-free paper.

TOTAL: ___ /45 = ___%

Comments:

Product Advertising

Criteria

1. What product is being advertised?

2. What colours are predominant, and what messages do these colours send?

3. What other aspects of the advertisement other than colour contribute to the ad? Explain.

4. Who is the probable target audience? What tells you this?

5. What subconscious message about the product is being sent?

6. Is the ad effective? Why or why not?

—Assessment sheet for assignment 5 (self- or peer-assessment)

Analysis of a Character

Mechanics

5   Virtually an error-free poem. The few minor mistakes do not take away from the overall quality of the poem.

4   Errors are minimal. Still a high quality of writing.

3   Errors are present and hinder the quality of the poem at times.

2   Errors are too plentiful. Errors hinder understanding on many occasions.

1   Errors are too abundant and totally take away from the understanding of the poem.

Word Choice and Figurative Devices (x 2)

5   Word choice and use of figurative devices are specific and enhance the poem to make it extremely effective.

4   Word choice and use of figurative language are thoughtful and effective on many occasions.

3   Word choice is general rather than specific. Some figurative devices are attempted.

2   Word choice is too general and lacks thought. Words are used incorrectly on occasion. Little or no attempt to incorporate figurative devices.

1   Word choice is non-creative and ineffective. Words are used incorrectly. No evidence of figurative devices.

Thought and Detail (x 2)

5   Ideas are unique and insightful. Strong evidence of synthesizing material from the novel. You have gone well beyond the plot and demonstrate complex thought.

4   Ideas are thoughtful and interesting. Evidence of synthesizing material from the novel. You have gone beyond the plot and make thoughtful comments about characterization.

2   Ideas are general rather than specific. General ideas and points taken from the novel.

2   Ideas are vague at times. Inconsistent with the novel at times, and there are undeveloped ideas.

1   Ideas are ineffective. Inconsistent with the novel much of the time, and there is little or no development of ideas from the novel.

Visual Representation (x 2)

5   Meaningful and imaginative use of imagery, colour, texture, and juxtaposition.

4   Graphically effective use of imagery, colour, texture, and juxtaposition.

3   Functional use of imagery, colour, texture, and juxtaposition.

2   Weak use of imagery, colour, texture, and juxtaposition.

1   Ineffective use of imagery, colour, texture, and juxtaposition (or lacking altogether).

TOTAL: _____ /35 marks = _____%

Comments:

Studying a Novel

Thought and Detail (x 2.5)

5   Theme is insightfully addressed. Images and symbols keenly enhance the thematic development. The five quotes are astutely integrated.

4   Theme is thoughtfully addressed. Images and symbols specifically enhance the thematic development. The five quotes are carefully integrated.

3   Theme is generally addressed. Images and symbols are present but could reflect the theme more strongly. The five quotes are included but are general rather than specific.

2   Theme is vaguely addressed (obscure at times). Images and symbols are lacking or do not reflect the theme effectively. Quotes are either obscure or lacking in numbers.

1   Theme is uncertain (or not addressed at all). Images and symbols do not enhance the theme or are contradictory to the theme. Quotes are deficient in number or have little or no relevance in developing the theme.

Organization (x 1.5)

5   Unique method of displaying the information. The form and composition clearly enhance the ideas presented.

4   Interesting method of displaying the information. The form and composition strongly develop the ideas presented.

3   Appropriate method of displaying the information. The form and composition develop the ideas presents.

2   Weak method of displaying information. The form and composition lack sense of organization and purpose.

1   Deficient method of displaying information. The form and composition do not contribute to the ideas presented.

Matters of Choice (x 2.5)

5   Meaningful and imaginative use of imagery, colour, texture, and juxtaposition.

4   Graphically effective use of imagery, colour, texture, and juxtaposition.

3   Functional use of imagery, colour, texture, and juxtaposition.

2   Ineffective use of imagery, colour, texture, and juxtaposition.

1   Poor or lack of use of imagery, colour, texture, and juxtaposition.

TOTAL: _____ /32.5 = _____ %

Comments:

—Rubric for assignment 7

Watching a Movie Worksheet

You have just viewed an important movie and now will write an essay about it.

Movie Title: _____

Producer: _____

Director: _____

Actors: _____

Brief overview of the movie:

What is the historical and/or political message in the movie?

What is the link between the movie and the future as you see it?

Watching a Movie

Thought and Detail (x 2)

5   Ideas are unique and insightful. Strong evidence of synthesizing material from the movie. You have gone well beyond the plot and demonstrate complex thought.

4   Ideas are thoughtful and interesting. Evidence of synthesizing material from the movie. You have gone beyond the plot and make thoughtful comments about them.

3   Ideas are general rather than specific. General ideas and points taken from the the movie.

2   Ideas are vague at times. Inconsistent with the movie at times, and ideas undeveloped.

1   Ideas are ineffective. Inconsistent with the movie much of the time, and there is little or no development of ideas from the movie.

Word Choice and Figurative Devices (x 2)

5   Word choice and use of figurative devices are specific and enhance the essay to make it extremely effective.

4   Word choice and use of figurative language are thoughtful and effective on many occasions.

3   Word choice is general rather than specific. Some figurative devices attempted.

2   Word choice is too general and lacks thought. Words are used incorrectly on occasion. Little or no attempt to incorporate figurative devices.

1   Word choice is non-creative and ineffective. Words are used incorrectly. No evidence of figurative devices.

Mechanics

5   Virtually an error-free essay. The few minor mistakes do not take away from the overall quality of the essay.

4   Errors are minimal. Still a high quality of writing.

3   Errors are present and hinder the quality of the essay at times.

2   Errors are too plentiful. Errors hinder understanding on many occasions.

1   Errors are too abundant and totally take away from the understanding of the essay.

TOTAL: _____ /25 = _____ %

Comments:

Conducting an Interview

The Likert Scale: 1 – poor; 2 – fair; 3 – satisfactory; 4 – very good; 5 – superior

1. Research: Depth of information used in the interview or event.

    1   2   3   4   5

2. Questions: Quality of the prepared questions asked of the historical character; clarity and smoothness of the transition.

    1   2   3   4   5

3. Responses: Quality of the historical figure's responses.

    1   2   3   4   5

4. Concepts: Quality of the development of major ideas.

    1   2   3   4   5

5. Presentation: Quality of the presentation of ideas and format.

    1   2   3   4   5

Comments:

Bibliography

Alvermann, D. *Effective Literacy Instruction for Adolescents.* Executive
    Summary and Paper Commissioned by the National Reading
    Conference. Chicago: National Reading Conference, 2001.

Anderson, L.H. *Speak.* New York: Puffin, 2001.

Andrasick, K. *Opening Texts: Using Writing to Teach Literature.* Portsmouth,
    NH: Heinemann, 1990.

Applebee, A. *Contexts for Learning to Write: Studies of Secondary School
    Instruction.* Norwood, NJ: Ablex, 1984.

Atwell, N. *In the Middle: New Understandings about Writing, Reading, and
    Literature.* 2nd ed. Toronto: Irwin, 1998.

Augsburger, D. "Teacher as Writer: Remembering the Agony, Sharing
    the Ecstasy." *Journal of Adolescent and Adult Literacy* 41.7 (1998):
    548–552.

Banus, M. "Eighteen." *A Book of Women Poets: From Antiquity to Now.* New
    York: Schocken, 1992.

Black, P., C. Harrison, C. Lee, B. Marshall, and D. William. *Assessment for
    Learning: Putting It into Practice.* New York: Open UP, 2003.

Bradbury, R. *Bradbury Speaks: Too Soon from the Cave, Too Far from the
    Stars.* Rpt. ed. New York: Harper Perennial, 2006.

Bright, R. *Writing Instruction in the Intermediate Grades: What Is Said,
    What Is Done, What Is Understood.* Newark, DE: International Reading
    Association, 1995.

_____. *Write from the Start: Writers Workshop in the Primary Grades.*
    Winnipeg: Portage and Main, 2000.

Bright, R., L. McMullin, and D. Platt. *From Your Child's Teacher: Helping
    a Child Learn to Read, Write, and Speak Effectively.* Stettler, AB: F.P.
    Hendriks, 1998.

Brooks, K. *Lucas.* Toronto: Scholastic Paperbacks, 2004.

Brooks, T. *The Sword of Shannara Trilogy.* London, UK: Orbit, 2002.

Bruce, B. "Diversity and Critical Social Engagement: How Changing
    Technologies Enable New Modes of Literacy in Changing
    Circumstances." *Adolescents and Literacies in a Digial World.* Ed. D.
    Alvermann. New York: Peter Lang, 2002. 1–18.

Burdett, L. *Romeo and Juliet: For Kids.* Shakespeare Can Be Fun Series.
    Richmond Hill, ON: Firefly, 1998.

Butler, R. "Enhancing and Undermining Intrinsic Motivation: The Effects of Task-Involving and Ego-Involving Evaluation on Interest and Performance." *British Journal of Educational Psychololgy* 58 (1988): 1–14.

Coville, B. *William Shakespeare's* A Midsummer Night's Dream. [Retold by Bruce Coville] New York: Puffin, 1996.

Crowe, C. "A Comparison of Elements of Writing Considered Important by Professional Writers and Composition Textbooks." Diss. Arizona State University, 1986.

Dickens, C. *A Tale of Two Cities.* 1859. Signet Classics, 1997.

Dyson, A.H. *Social Worlds of Children Learning to Write in an Urban Primary School.* New York: Teachers College Press, 1992.

Elbow, P. *Everyone Can Write.* New York: Oxford UP, 2000.

Ellis, D. *Looking for X.* Vancouver: Groundwood, 2001.

Emig, J. *The Composing Processes of Twelfth Graders.* Urbana, IL: National Conference of Teachers of English, 1971.

English, K. "Excelling at Young Writer 101." Interview with Steven Galloway." *Globe and Mail* 4 May 2003: R4.

Fiderer, A. *Rubrics: Scoring Guidelines for Performance Assessment.* 1996. Accessed 20 February 2007. <http://teacher.scholastic.com/professional/profdev/summerbookclubs/grade46/s3_topic1.htm>.

Fletcher, R., and J.A. Portalupi. *Writing Workshop: The Essential Guide.* Portsmouth, NH: Heinemann, 2001.

Flower, L., and J. Hayes. "Plans that Guide the Composing Process." *Writing: Process, Development, and Communication.* Ed. C. Frederiksen and J. Dominic. Hillsdale, NJ: Lawrence Erlbaum, 1981. 39–58.

Forsyth, F. *The Day of the Jackal.* New York: Bantam, 1982.

Goldberg, N. *Writing Down the Bones.* Boston: Shambhala, 1986.

____. N. *Thunder and Lightning: Cracking Open the Writer's Craft.* New York: Bantam, 2000.

Golding, W. *Lord of the Flies.* New York: Perigee Trade, 1959.

Graves, D.H. *Writing: Teachers and Children at Work.* Portsmouth, NH: Heinemann, 1983.

Gundlach, R. "On the Nature and Development of Children's Writing." *Writing: Process, Development, and Communication.* Ed. C. Frederiksen and J. Dominic. Hillsdale, NJ: Lawrence Erlbaum, 1981. 133–152.

Hillocks, George, Jr. *Research on Written Composition: New Directions for Teaching.* Urbana, IL: ERIC Clearinghouse on Reading and Communication Skills and the National Conference on Research in English, 1986.

Hinton, S.E. *The Outsiders.* New York: Puffin, 1997.

Holeman, L. *Saying Good-Bye.* Toronto: Lester, 1995.

____. *Devil's Darning Needle.* Erin, ON: Porcupine's Quill, 1999.

____. *Raspberry House Blues.* Toronto: Tundra, 2000.

____. *The Linnet Bird.* London, UK: Headline, 2004.

Howard, J. *Writing to Learn.* Washington, DC: Council of Basic Education, 1983.

Hughes, E. *Writing from the Inner Self.* New York: HarperCollins, 1984.

Juby, S. *Alice, I Think.* Toronto: HarperCollins, 2000.

Kellogg, S. *Jack and the Beanstalk.* New York: Morrow, 1991.

King, S. *Dreamcatcher*. New York: Scribner, 2001.

Kingsolver, B. *Small Wonder*. New York: Perennial, 2002.

Kittle, P. "Writing Giants, Columbine, and the Queen of Route 16." *Voices from the Middle* 9.1 (2001): 8–11.

Koran, C. *Teaching Film as Literature: A Teacher's Guide*. Lethbridge, AB: privately published, 2003.

Lamott, A. *Bird by Bird: Some Instructions on Writing and Life*. New York: Anchor, 1994.

Langer, J., and A. Applebee. *How Writing Shapes Thinking: A Study of Teaching and Learning*. Urbana, IL: National Council of Teachers of English, 1987.

Lindemann, E. *A Rhetoric for Writing Teachers*. New York: Oxford UP, 2001.

Lodge, D. *Consciousness and the Novel*. Cambridge, MA: Harvard UP, 2002.

Marshall, J. *Goldilocks and the Three Bears*. Toronto: Fitzhenry and Whiteside, 1988.

McCourt, F. *Angela's Ashes: A Memoir*. New York: Scribner, 1999.

Murray, D. "Internal Revision: A Process of Discovery." *Research on Composing: Points of Departure*. Ed. C.R. Cooper and L. Odell. Urbana, IL: National Council of Teachers of English, 1978. 85–103.

____. "Writing as Process: How Writing Finds its Own Meaning." *Eight Approaches to Teaching Composition*. Ed. R. Donovan and B. McClelland. Urbana, IL: National Council of Teachers of English, 1980. 3–20.

____. *A Writer Teaches Writing*. 2nd ed. Boston: Houghton Mifflin, 1985.

____. *Learning by Teaching: Selected Articles on Writing and Teaching*. Upper Montclair, NJ: Boynton/Cook, 1982.

Narter, D. "Teacher as Machine: The Cost of Objectivity." *English Journal* 94.4 (2005): 65–69.

National Council of Teachers of English (NCTE). *Beliefs about the Teaching of Writing*. Urbana, IL: National Council of Teachers of English, 2004.

Noskin, D. "Teaching Writing in the High School: Fifteen Years in the Making." *English Journal* 90.1 (2000): 34–38.

Ogle, D. "K-W-L: A Teaching Model that Develops Active Reading of Expository Text." *The Reading Teacher* 39 (1986): 564–570.

Paolini, C. *Eragon*. New York: Knopf Books for Young Readers, 2000.

____. "Author Spotlight." 1995. Accessed 20 February 2007. < randomhouse.com/author/results.pperl?authorid:543888view: fullsptlght > .

Peterson, S. *Becoming Better Writers*. Edmonton: F.P. Hendriks, 1995.

Pressley, M. "The Need for Research on Secondary Literacy Education." *Adolescent Literacy Research and Practice*. Ed. T. Jetton and J. Dole. New York: Guildford, 2004. 415–432.

Pullman, P. *His Dark Materials, Part I: The Golden Compass*. New York: Alfred A. Knopf, 1996.

Rief, L. "Doing the Write Thing." *Voices from the Middle* 12.1 (2004): 58–59.

Saddler, B. "'But Teacher, I Added a Period!' Middle Schoolers Learn to Revise." *Voices from the Middle* 11.2 (2003): 20–26.

Scieszka, J. *Frog Prince Continued*. New York: Viking, 1991.

Shanahan, T. "Overcoming the Dominance of Communication: Writing to Think and to Learn." *Adolescent Literacy Research and Practice*. Ed. T. Jetton and J. Dole. New York: Guilford, 2004. 59–74.

Smede, S. "Interior Design: Revision as Focus." *English Journal* 90.1 (2000): 117–121.

Smith, F. *Writing and the Writer*. New York: Holt, Rinehart, and Winston, 1982.

Spinelli, J. *Stargirl*. New York: Random House, 2000.

Swartzendruber-Putnam, D. "Written Reflection: Creating Better Thinkers, Better Writers. *English Journal* 90.1 (2000): 88–93.

Tompkins, G., R. Bright, M. Pollard, and P. Winsor. *Language Arts: Content and Teaching Strategies*. Scarborough, ON: Pearson Education, 2007.

Ueland, Brenda. 1938. *If You Want to Write: A Book about Art, Independence, and Spirit*. St. Paul, MN: Graywolf, 1997.

VanDeWeghe, R. "'Awesome, Dude!' Responding Helpfully to Peer Writing." *English Journal* 94.1: 95–99.

Vygotsky, L. *Thought and Language*. Cambridge, MA: MIT Press, 1986.

Wiesel, E. *Night*. New York: Hill and Wang, 2006.

Wilcox, B. "Writing Portfolios: Active vs. Passive." *English Journal* 86.6 (1997): 34–37.

Wolf, S., and K. Wolf. "Teaching True and to the Test in Writing." *Language Arts* 79.3 (2002): 229–240.

Wotring, A., and R. Tierney. *Two Studies of Writing in High School Science*. Classroom Research Study No. 5. Berkeley, CA: Bay Area Writing Project, 1981.